The Charlton Standard Catalogue

First World War Canadian Corps Badges

1ST EDITION

W. K. CROSS
Publisher

AL ROSEN
Pricing Editor

The Charlton Press
TORONTO, ONTARIO • BIRMINGHAM, MICHIGAN

COPYRIGHT AND TRADEMARK NOTICE

Copyright © 1995 Charlton International Inc. All rights reserved.

The terms Charlton, Charlton's, The Charlton Press, the Charlton Cataloguing System, Charlton Numbers and abbreviations thereof, are trademarks of Charlton International Inc. and shall not be used without written consent from Charlton International Inc.

While every care has been taken to ensure accuracy in the compilation of the data in this catalogue, the publisher cannot accept responsibility for typographical errors.

No part of this publication may be reproduced, stored in a retrieval system, or transmitted in any form or by any means, electronic, mechanical, photocopying, recording, or otherwise without the prior written permission of the copyright owner.

No copyright material may be used without written permission in each instance from Charlton International Inc. Permission will be liberally given for the use of the CHARLTON CATALOGUE NUMBERING SYSTEM by anyone wishing to do so, including its uses in advertisments of items for sale provided Charlton receives proper acknowledgement in each instance.

Permission is hereby given for brief excerpts to be used for the purpose of reviewing this publication in newspapers, magazines, periodicals and bulletins, other than in the advertising of items for sale, provided the source of the material so used is acknowledged in each instance.

Canadian Cataloguing in Publication Data
Main entry under title:
The Charlton standard catalogue of First
World War Canadian Corps badges
1991-
Biennial.
Description based on: 1st. ed.
ISSN 0706-0424
ISBN 0-8968-162-7 (1st ed.)
1. Canada. Canadian Army--Infantry--Insignia--
Catalogs. 2. Badges--Canada--Catalogs.
UC535.C3C42   355.1'4   C94-900410-3

**Printed in Canada
in the Province of Ontario**

The Charlton Press

**Editorial Office
2010 Yonge Street
Toronto, Ontario M4S 1Z9
Telephone (416) 488-4653 Fax: (416) 488-4656
Telephone (800) 442-6042 Fax: (800) 442-1542**

EDITORIAL

Editor	W. K. Cross
Pricing Editor	Al Rosen
Editorial Assistant	Jean Dale
Editorial Assistant	Davina Rowan
Editorial Assistant	Sandra Tooze
Layout	Marc Rowan
Cover Photography	David MacFadyen

ACKNOWLEDGEMENTS

The Charlton Press wishes to thank all those who have assisted in this First Edition of The Charlton Standard Catalogue of First World War Canadian Corps Badges. In particular we would like to recognize:

John Anderton, C. G. Brooker, Edward Denby, J. R. G. Edwards, Jeffrey Hoare, Stephen M. Pallas, Robert I. Rolleg, Gary Roncetti, Robert J. Russell and L. T. Wood.

ABOUT THE PRICING IN THIS CATALOGUE

The purpose of this catalogue is to give the most accurate, up-to-date retail prices for all First World War Canadian Corps badges. These prices are drawn from both dealer and collector activity, recent auction results and are averaged to reflect the current marketplace for Infantry badges.

A necessary word of caution. No catalogue can or should propose to be a fixed price list. Collector interest, badge rarity factors and other vagaries of the hobby itself invariably dictate time of transaction retail values.

This catalogue then, should be considered as a guide, showing the most accurate current retail prices possible for the collector and dealer alike.

Our pricing editor, Al Rosen, invites correspondence with collectors and dealers on pricing information for the 2nd edition. Please write to him at: 211 Yonge Street, Suite 200A, Toronto, Ontario, M5B 1M4.

GEORGE F. HEMSLEY CO. LIMITED, MANUFACTURERS :: MONTREAL

CAP AND COLLAR BADGES

2nd Overseas Mounted Rifles
Montreal

5th Overseas Mounted Rifles
Sherbrooke

6th Overseas Mounted Rifles
New Brunswick

CAP AND COLLAR BADGES

9th Overseas Mounted Rifles
Alberta

12th Overseas Mounted Rifles
Calgary

13th Overseas Mounted Rifles
Alberta

TABLE OF CONTENTS

Introductory Note xiii
Condition xiii
Major Varieties xiii
Minor Varieties xiii
Manufacturers xiv
Fasteners xv
Finishes xv
Composition xv
Numbering System xvi

5 CANADIAN ARMY VETERINARY CORPS
Maple Leaf Design 1
Wreath of Maple Leaves ---- Open 2
Wreath of Maple Leaves ---- Closed 3

10 THE CANADIAN CAVALRY CORPS
1ST CANADIAN CAVALRY BRIGADE
Royal Canadian Dragoons 4
Lord Strathcona's Horse (Royal Canadians) 5
Fort Garry Horse 6
2ND CANADIAN CAVALRY BRIGADE
Mounted Rifle Brigade 7
THE CANADIAN LIGHT HORSE
Royal North West Mounted Police 8
1st Hussars 9
19th Alberta Dragoons 10
16th Canadian Light Horse 11
CANADIAN MOUNTED RIFLE BATTALIONS
1st Mounted Rifle Battalion 12
2nd Mounted Rifle Battalion
With Brackets Around "B.C.H." 13
Without Brackets Around "B.C.H." 14
3rd Mounted Rifle Battalion 15
4th Mounted Rifle Battalion
C.M.R. Design 16
C.M.R.R. Design 17
5th Mounted Rifle Battalion 18
6th Mounted Rifle Battalion 19
7th Mounted Rifle Battalion 20
8th Mounted Rifle Battalion 21
9th Mounted Rifle Battalion 22
10th Mounted Rifle Battalion 23
11th Mounted Rifle Battalion 24
12th Mounted Rifle Battalion 25
13th Mounted Rifle Battalion 26
CANADIAN MOUNTED RIFLE DRAFT 27

15 CANADIAN CORPS
CANADIAN MILITARY HEADQUARTERS 28
CORPS OF MILITARY STAFF CLERKS 29
DEPARTMENT OF THE GENERAL AUDITOR 30
INSTRUCTIONAL TROOPS
Canadian School of Musketry 31
Canadian Physical Instructors 32

20 CANADIAN CORPS CYCLISTS
General Service Badge 33

DIVISIONAL CYCLISTS COMPANIES
   1st Divisional Cyclist Company 34
   2nd Divisional Cyclist Company
      Wheel Design 35
      Maple Leaf Design 36
   3rd Divisional Cyclist Company 37
   4th Divisional Cyclist Company 38
   5th Divisional Cyclist Company 39
CANADIAN CYCLIST DRAFT 40

25 CANADIAN DEPOT BATTALIONS
Alberta Regiment
   1st Depot Battalion 41
British Columbia Regiment
   1st Depot Battalion 42
   2nd Depot Battalion 43
Manitoba Regiment
   1st Depot Battalion 44
New Brunswick Regiment
   1st Depot Battalion 45
Nova Scotia Regiment
   1st Depot Battalion 46
   Regimental Depot 47
1st Central Ontario Regiment
   1st Depot Battalion 48
   2nd Depot Battalion 48
2nd Central Ontario Regiment
   1st Depot Battalion 49
   2nd Depot Battalion 49
Eastern Ontario Regiment
   1st Depot Battalion 50
   2nd Depot Battalion 50
Western Ontario Regiment
   1st Depot Battalion 51
1st Quebec Regiment
   1st Depot Battalion, French Legends 52
   1st Depot Battalion, English Legends 53
   2nd Depot Battalion 53
2nd Quebec Regiment
   1st Depot Battalion, French Legends 54
   1st Depot Battalion, English Legends 55
   2nd Depot Battalion, French Legends 56
   2nd Depot Battalion, English Legends 57
   3rd Depot Battalion 57
Saskatchewan Regiment
   1st Depot Battalion 58

30 THE CANADIAN FORESTRY CORPS
General Service Badges
   Without "Overseas" 59
   With "Overseas" 60
   Piper's Badge 60
CANADIAN FORESTRY BATTALIONS
General Service Badges
   Tree and Axe Design 61
   Modified 238th Infantry Battalion 62
   Tree and Saw Design 62
224th Infantry Battalion 63
238th Infantry Battalion 64
CANADIAN FORESTRY COMPANIES
1st Forestry Company 65
2nd Forestry Company 66
12th Forestry Company 67
50th Forestry Company 68
70th Forestry Company 69

	British Columbia Forestry Company ... 69
	Manitoba Forestry Company ... 70
	New Brunswick Forestry Company
	"N.B." Overlaid on Tiptaft General Service Badge ... 71
	"N.B." Overlaid on 238th Battalion Badge ... 71
	Nova Scotia Forestry Company ... 72
	Quebec Forestry Company ... 73
35	CANADIAN GARRISON REGIMENTS AND BATTALIONS
	Canadian Garrison Regiment ... 74
	British Columbia Garrison Regiment ... 75
	4th Garrison Battalion ... 76
40	THE CANADIAN INTELLIGENCE CORPS
	General Service Badge ... 77
45	THE CANADIAN MACHINE GUN CORPS
	General Service Badge
	Imperial Issue ... 78
	Canadian Issue --- Style A ... 79
	Canadian Issue --- Style B ... 80
	Canadian Issue --- Style C ... 81
	Canadian Issue --- Style D ... 82
	CANADIAN MACHINE GUN COMPANIES
	1st Machine Gun Company ... 83
	2nd Machine Gun Company ... 83
	3rd Machine Gun Company ... 84
	4th Machine Gun Company ... 85
	5th Machine Gun Company ... 85
	6th Machine Gun Company ... 85
	9th Machine Gun Company ... 86
	NEW BRUNSWICK MACHINE GUN DRAFT ... 87
50	CANADIAN MOTOR MACHINE GUN BRIGADES
	1ST CANADIAN MOTOR MACHINE GUN BRIGADE ... 88
	Borden's Motor Machine Gun Battery ... 89
	2ND CANADIAN MOTOR MACHINE GUN BRIGADE
	Eaton's Motor Machine Gun Battery ... 90
	Maple Leaf Cross Guns Design ... 91
	Boyle's Yukon Motor Machine Gun Battery ... 92
	CANADIAN MOTOR MACHINE GUN BRIGADE
	Miscellaneous Shoulder Titles ... 93
55	CANADIAN MILITARY, YMCA
	YOUNG MEN'S CHRISTIAN ASSOCIATION
	Canadian Design ... 95
	PX Design ... 95
	YMCA Military Service ... 94
60	THE CANADIAN PROVOST CORPS
	CANADIAN MILITARY POLICE CORPS
	"CMP" Cypher Design ... 96
	"GVR" Cypher Design ... 97
	CANADIAN MILITARY POLICE DETACHMENT
	1st Detachment ... 98
	THE SPECIAL SERVICES COMPANIES
	2nd Special Service Company
	Without "C.E.F." Design ... 99
	With "C.E.F." Design ... 100
	3rd Special Service Company ... 100
	4th Special Service Company ... 101
	12th Special Service Company ... 101

65 THE CORPS OF CANADIAN RAILWAY TROOPS
CANADIAN OVERSEAS RAILWAY CONSTRUCTION CORPS
General Service Badge 102
CANADIAN CONSTRUCTION BATTALIONS
1st Battalion 103
2nd Battalion 104
3rd Battalion
    239th Battalion Badge 105
    Modified 239th Battalion Badge 106
CANADIAN RAILWAY TROOPS
1st Battalion 107
2nd Battalion (127th Infantry) 108
3rd Battalion 110
4th Battalion 111
5th Battalion
    Wreath of Maple Leaves Design 112
    Maple Leaf Design 113
6th Battalion
    Grenade Design 114
    Maple Leaf Design 115
7th Battalion
    Oval Design 116
    Maple Leaf on Crowned Annulus Design 117
8th Battalion 118
9th Battalion 119
10th Battalion
    256th Battalion Badge 120
    Modified 256th Interim Badge 121
    Railway Tunnel Design 122
    Maple Leaf Design 123
11th Battalion 124
12th Battalion 125
13th Battalion 126
CANADIAN RAILWAY TROOPS DEPOT 127
1ST BRIDGING COMPANY 128
SKILLED RAILWAY EMPLOYEES
No. 1 Section 129
No. 2 Section 130
No. 3 Section 131
No. 4 Section 132
70 THE CORPS OF ROYAL CANADIAN ENGINEERS
CANADIAN ENGINEERS
General Service Badge 133
CANADIAN PIONEER BATTALIONS
1st Pioneer Battalion 134
2nd Pioneer Battalion 135
3rd Pioneer Battalion 136
4th Pioneer Battalion 137
5th Pioneer Battalion 138
107th Pioneer Battalion 139
123rd Pioneer Battalion 140
124th Pioneer Battalion 142
PIONEER DRAFT 143
PIONEER TRAINING DEPOT 144
CANADIAN LABOUR BATTALIONS
4th Labour Battalion 145
CANADIAN LABOUR COMPANY 146
INFANTRY WORKS COMPANIES
1st Infantry Works Company 147
2nd Infantry Works Company 148

	3rd Infantry Works Company	148
	4th Infantry Works Company	149
75	**THE ROYAL CANADIAN ARMOURED CORPS**	
	CANADIAN TANK CORPS	
	General Service Badge	150
	Interim Badge	151
	Interim Badge	152
	CANADIAN TANK BATTALIONS	
	1st Tank Battalion	153
	2nd Tank Battalion	154
	3rd Tank Battalion	155
	CANADIAN TANK CORPS TRAINING INSTRUCTORS	156
80	**THE ROYAL CANADIAN ARMY CHAPLAIN CORPS**	
	CANADIAN CHAPLAIN SERVICE	
	General Service Badges	
	Cross and Maple Leaf Design	157
	Plain Framed Cross	158
	Maple Leaves in the Arms of a Framed Cross	159
	Square Stylized Cross	159
	SALVATION ARMY CHAPLAIN SERVICE	
	Blood and Fire Design with Ribbon	160
	Blood and Fire Design without Ribbon	160
85	**THE ROYAL CANADIAN ARMY MEDICAL CORPS**	
	CANADIAN ARMY MEDICAL CORPS	
	General Service Badge	161
	CANADIAN STATIONARY HOSPITALS	
	8th Stationary Hospital	162
	9th Stationary Hospital	163
	CANADIAN CASUALTY CLEARING STATIONS	
	2nd Casualty Clearing Station	164
	CANADIAN FIELD AMBULANCES	
	1st Canadian Field Ambulance	165
	2nd Canadian Field Ambulance	
	Without "Overseas"	166
	With "Overseas"	167
	Interim Badge	168
	3rd Canadian Field Ambulance	169
	4th Canadian Field Ambulance	169
	8th Canadian Field Ambulance	170
	9th Canadian Field Ambulance	170
	10th Canadian Field Ambulance	171
90	**THE ROYAL CANADIAN ARMY PAY CORPS**	
	CANADIAN ARMY PAY CORPS	
	General Service Badges	
	Single Maple Leaf Design	172
	Six Maple Leaves Deisgn	173
95	**THE ROYAL CANADIAN ARMY SERVICE CORPS**	
	CANADIAN ARMY SERVICE CORPS	
	General Service Badge	174
	ARMY SERVICES COMPANIES	
	7th Company	175
	19th Company	175
	AMMUNITION SUB PARK COMPANIES	
	1st Ammunition Sub Park	176
	2nd Ammunition Sub Park	176
	3rd Ammunition Sub Park	177
	4th Ammunition Sub Park	177

DIVISIONAL TRAINS
  4th Train 178
AMMUNITION SUB PARK MECHANICAL TRANSPORT COMPANY 179
AMBULANCE WORKSHOPS
  4th Ambulance Workshop 180
ARMY SERVICE DEPOT COMPANIES
  8th (Overseas) Depot Unit of Supply 181
  21st (Overseas) Depot Unit of Supply 182
  Remount Depot 182
TRAINING DEPOTS
  1st Overseas Training Depot 183

100 THE ROYAL CANADIAN CORPS OF SIGNALS
  CANADIAN SIGNALS CORPS
    General Service Badge 184

105 THE ROYAL CANADIAN DENTAL CORPS
  CANADIAN ARMY DENTAL CORPS
    General Service Badge
      Error Legend 185
      Corrected Legend 186
      "CADA" Cypher Design 187

110 THE ROYAL CANADIAN HORSE ARTILLERY
    General Service Badge 188

125 THE ROYAL CANADIAN ORDNANCE CORPS
  CANADIAN ORDNANCE CORPS
    General Service Badge 189
    Canadian Arms Inspection Repair Depot 190

130 THE ROYAL CANADIAN POSTAL CORPS
  CANADIAN POSTAL CORPS
    General Service Badge 191

135 THE ROYAL FLYING CORPS
    General Service Badge 192

140 THE ROYAL REGIMENT OF CANADIAN ARTILLERY
  THE ROYAL CANADIAN GARRISON ARTILLERY
    General Service Badges
      Imperial Issue 193
      Modified Imperial Issue 194
      Canadian Issue — Style A 195
      Canadian Issue — Style B 196
      Canadian Issue — Style C 197
      Canadian Issue — Styel D 198

145 THE ROYAL CANADIAN FIELD ARTILLERY
  CANADIAN FIELD ARTILLERY
    General Service Badge
      Canadian Issue - Style B 199
      Miscellaneous Shoulder Titles 200
  OVERSEAS FIELD BATTERIES
    13th Brigade Headquaters 201
    13th Field Artillery Brigade Ammunition Column 202
    36th Overseas Field Battery 203
    46th Overseas Field Battery 204
    50th Overseas Field Battery 205
    51st Overseas Field Battery 206
    52nd Overseas Field Battery 207
    53rd Overseas Field Battery 208
    55th Overseas Field Battery 209
    56th Overseas Field Battery
      Standard Gun Badge 210

   Maple Leaf Badge 211
   57th Overseas Field Battery 212
   58th Overseas Field Battery 213
   61st Overseas Field Battery 214
   62nd Overseas Field Battery 215
   63rd Overseas Field Battery
    Standard Gun Badge 216
    Canada/63/Overseas Badge 217
   64th Overseas Field Battery
    Standard Gun Badge 218
    Maple Leaf Badge 219
   65th Overseas Field Battery 220
   66th Overseas Field Battery 221
   67th Overseas Field Battery 222
   68th Overseas Field Battery 223
   69th Overseas Field Battery 224
   70th Overseas Field Battery 225
   71st Overseas Field Battery 226
   72nd Overseas Field Battery 227
   73rd Overseas Field Battery 228
   74th Overseas Field Battery 229
   75th Overseas Field Battery 230
   76th Overseas Field Battery 231
   77th Overseas Field Battery 232
   78th Overseas Field Battery 233
   79th Overseas Field Battery
    Standard Gun Badge 234
    Grenade Badge 235
  TRAINING BATTERIES
   Standard Gun Badge
    Overlaid Numeral 236
    Overlaid Letter 237
150 CANADIAN CORPS HEAVY ARTILLERY
   3rd Overseas Siege Batteries
    With "Overseas" Battery 238
    Without "Overseas" Battery 239
   4th Overseas Siege Battery 240
   5th Overseas Siege Battery 240
   9th Overseas Siege Battery 241
   10th Overseas Siege Battery 242
   Heavy Artillery Draft Batteries
    5th P.E.I. Overseas Siege Artillery Draft 243
    King's Country Siege Artillery Draft 244
    McGill University Overseas Siege Artillery Draft
     "Over Seas" Two Words 245
     "Overseas" One Word 246
    Nova Scotia Overseas Siege Artillery Draft 247
  TRENCH MORTAR BATTERIES
   10th Trench Mortar Battery
    Maple Leaf Design 248
    Oval Design 249
   11th Trench Mortar Battery 249
  COBOURG HEAVY BATTERY DEPOT 250
  DIVISIONAL AMMUNITION COLUMNS
   1st Divisional Ammunition Column 251
   3rd Divisional Ammunition Column 252
   4th Divisional Ammunition Column 252
155 CANADIAN FIELD COMFORTS COMMISSION 253
160 IMPERIAL MUNITIONS BOARD 253
165 KHAKI UNIVERSITY OF CANADA 254

WHOLESALE LIST.

CANADA MILITARY BADGES.

These Badges are "Made in Canada," from the Official Dies, and are Strictly Regulation.

			Green Finish. doz.	Brown Finish. doz.	Brass. doz.
Canada Maple Leaf	Cap	Badge	8/3	7/6	
,,	Collar	Badges	9/9 pairs	9/- pairs	
,,	Titles	Solid	9/- ,,	7/6 ,,	7/6 pairs
,,	,,	Pierced	10/6 ,,	9/- ,,	9/- ,,
2nd Brigade Mounted Rifles	Cap	Badge	9/-	8/3	
	Collar	Badges	10/6 pairs	9/9 pairs	
Remount Depot	Cap	Badge	8/3	7/6	
,,	Collar	Badges	9/9 pairs	9/- pairs	
5th Mounted Rifles	Cap	Badge	8/3	7/6	
,,	Collar	Badges	9/9 pairs	9/- pairs	
6th Mounted Rifles	Cap	Badge	8/3	7/6	
,, (Right & left)	Collar	Badges	14/3 pairs	13/6 pairs	
9th Mounted Rifles	Cap	Badge	8/3	7/6	
,,	Collar	Badges	9/9 pairs	9 - pairs	
,,	Titles	Solid	16/6 ,,	15/- ,,	
10th Mounted Rifles	Titles	Pierced	16/6 ,,	15/- ,,	
12th Mounted Rifles	Cap	Badge	8/3	7/6	
,,	Collar	Badges	9/9 pairs	9/- pairs	
13th Mounted Rifles	Cap	Badge	9/-	8/3	
,,	Collar	Badges	10/6 pairs	9/9 pairs	
Bordens Motor Battery	Cap	Badge	22/6		
,,	Collar	Badges	27/6 pairs		
Canadian Artillery	Grenades		15/- ,,		
Officers Cap	Badge		20/-		
Rank & File Cap	Badge		7/6		5/-
C.F.A.	Titles		12/6 pairs	11/6 pairs	11/6 pairs
C.G.A.	Titles		12/6 ,,	11/6 ,,	11/6 ,,
Canadian Engineers	Grenades		15/-		
Infantry Battalions:— 24th, 26th, 28th, 38th, 40th, 49th, 55th, 56th, 60th, 61st, 64th,	Cap	Badge	8 3	7/6	
	Collar	Badges	9 9 pairs	9/- pairs	
41st, 44th, 45th, 51st, 65th, 69th, 77th, 82th.	Cap	Badge	9/-	8/3	
	Collar	Badges	10/6 pairs	9/9 pairs	
73rd Bat. Infantry	Collar	Badges	12/6 pairs		

			Green Finish. doz.	Brown Finish. doz.	Brass. doz.
Can. Army Service Corps	Cap	Badge	18/9		
	Collar	Badges	30/- pairs		
,, ,,	Titles	Pierced	24/- ,,		22/6 pairs
	Officers Cap		2 pieces	30/-	
	Officers Collar		2 pieces	45/- pairs	
Can. Army Medical Corps	Cap	Badge	18/9		
	Collar	Badges	30/ pairs		
	Officers Cap		2 pieces	30/-	
	Officers Collar		2 pieces	45/- pairs	
Canadian Chaplains	Cap	Badge	20/-		
,,	Collar	Badges	30/- pairs		

Swagger Canes (Real polished Maple with Miniature Badge in relief on top)
Canadian Maple Leaf
38th, 40th, 41st, 44th, 55th, 56th, 60th, 61st, 64th, 65th, 69th, 73rd, 82nd, 87th   12/6

    12/6

SOUVENIR BROOCHES, &c.

Made from the Collar Badge Dies, fitted with strong serviceable catch and pin:—

Canada Maple Leaf, C.A.S.C., C.A.M.C. Artillery Grenade, Engineer Grenade, Chaplains, Any Mounted Rifle or Infantry Battalion mentioned above, Canada Titles Solid, Canada Titles Pierced.

Green Finish, 5/3 doz.   Brown Finish, 4/6 doz.   Oxidized Silver 6/- doz Gold Plate, 7/6 doz.

Prices of above in Solid Sterling Silver, 20/-. Price in Solid Gold on application.

STERLING SILVER MINIATURE BADGES.   ⅜-in. high.

Made for 38th, 40th, 41st, 44th, 55th, 56th, 60th, 61st, 64th, 65th 69th, 73rd, 82nd, 87th Battalions only. Also Canada Maple Leaf.

Scarf Pins, oxidized	...	5/- dox.
Safety Pins, oxidized	...	6/- ,,
Dumbell Cuff Links	...	22/6 ,,
Loose Cuff Links	...	42/6 ,,

Prices of above in 10 carat Solid Gold on application.

TERMS : Cash, no discount. Whilst the rate of Bank Exchange is against Canada, a small additional premium will be charged, or checks on Canada at 4.88 to the £ accepted.

ORDERS CABLED to Canada free of charge to purchaser.

Correspondence Invited about any Badges not mentioned above.

GEO. F. HEMSLEY CO. LTD. (MONTREAL)

67, NEW OXFORD STREET, LONDON, W.C.

F. D. HENDERSON, Manager.   *In stock here 35 Cap Badges Green } Bordens Motor 28 pairs Collar Badges Green } Battery*

INTRODUCTORY NOTE

Finally, the corps badge book is a reality, the second in the C.E.F. series, which now completes the World War I listings. We have carried the numbering system of the infantry book forward to this book, in order that continuity in the books and the badges be maintained. These listings may be difficult to follow at first, but but as soon as one understands the different characteristics of the makers, the listings will add a new dimension to the collecting of C.E.F. badges.

As with all new catalogues, there will be errors and omissions. We do welcome your comments and insight on how we can improve future editions. If you have new information we would appreciate hearing from you.

CONDITION

A discussion on condition flows against the concept of something that by order was meant to be cleaned and polished. Is it correct to classify, in this case, by price for quality? It certainly is for officers versus other ranks, as in most cases there is a major quality difference in design and manufacture, and this must be indicated by a price difference. If a collection is built around the desire to have a series of original mint badges, then it is only fair that the value must be placed on condition, for as with anything else there are fewer high quality items than low quality. In the first edition we priced in two grades. In the second we have listed one insignia in E.F. (extremely fine) condition, leaving out mint. We are leaving the definitions in the first edition for we still feel that the collector may be willing to pay a slight premium for a mint badge, but not sufficiently and often to merit a mint pricing category.

MINT: As the word implies, straight from the makers. The badge will have full factory finish, original lugs and no part or section of the badge will be missing or replaced.

EXTREMELY FINE: The badge will have 50 to 75% of the original finish. No part or section of the badge will be missing or replaced. One or two of the original lugs may be replaced. The replacement, however, must not alter the original design concept of the badge.

MAJOR VARIETIES

The following criteria were used to define major varieties of a C.E.F. badge:

1. A new or completely different rendition of a major device used on the cap, collar or shoulder title.
2. Any change in the legend carried on the cap badge.

The maple leaf is one device that varies between makers, but we have considered that difference to be only minor and not to be classified within a major catagory.

MINOR VARIETIES

The following criteria were used to define major varieties of a C.E.F. badge:

1. Small variations in design between makers.
2. Small variations between dies of the same maker.
3. Different finishes.
4. Different metal composition.

We have attempted to record all the minor varieties that exist in the badges of the Canadian infantry of World War I, however, it is probable that we have missed some and hope that future editions will capture those missed.

MANUFACTURERS

The following list of makers will illustrate how extensive the manufacturing of C.E.F. insignia was during 1914-1918 period:

CANADIAN MANUFACTURERS

O. B. Allen	Jacoby
J. D. Bailey	Jackson
Birks	Kinnear & Desterre
D. E. Black	Geo. H. Lees
Caron Bros.	Maybees
Chauncey Maybees	McDougall
F. W. Coates	Patterson Bros.
Cook	D. A. Reesor
Creighton's	Reynolds
Dingley	Roden Bros.
Dingwall	Rosenthal
Ellis Bros.	Wm. Scully
J R. Gaunt & Son Ltd. (Montreal)	Stanley & Aylward
G. F. Hemsleys	Wellings
Inglis	Wheatley

UNITED STATES MANUFACTURERS

Service Supply Company

GREAT BRITAIN MANUFACTURERS

Brown	Hicks
Firmin & Son	Reiche
J. R. Gaunt Son Ltd.	Tiptaft Ltd.
Goldsmiths & Silversmiths Company Ltd.	

It is not clear whether all the makers listed above actually manufactured badges. In some cases a cap badge may appear with two raised or incused names on the back, such as "INGLIS/BLACK." Did this mean that Inglis struck the badges for Black? Further research is definitely required on makers.

FASTENERS

The method by which the metal insignia was attached to the clothing. Different styles used: Lugs, tangs, slide and pin

FINISHES

Badge finishes: The coating applied over the raw metal of the badge.

This seems to be a matter of personal preference by the commanding officer of the battalion when ordering badges. So far we have been unable to determine if there was a set of criteria by which the choice of finish could be selected.

The following finishes could be used:

    Pickled (khaki): Greenish-brown coating of enamel
    Browning: Light brown coating of enamel to give the appearance of bronze to match the uniform colour (sometimes referred to as bronze)
    Black: Black coating of enamel
    Antique: Brown/black coating of enamel
    Nickel Plating: Nickel over copper, brass, etc.
    Silver Plating: Silver over copper, brass, etc.
    Gilt: Gold over silver, copper, etc.

COMPOSITION

The composition of the C.E.F. insignia is straight foward for the only requirement was to produce a clean, clear impression of the chosen design in metal.

Metals compositions most used were:

    Other Ranks: Copper, brass, white metal
    Officers: Gilt, bronze, silver, gold, silver-plate on copper or brass on copper or brass

NUMBERING SYSTEM

In this book, the *The Charlton Standard Catalogue of First World War Canadian Corps Badges*, first edition, we have continued to develop a numbering system that will be useful in cataloguing the numerous varieties of C.E.F. badges, both infantry and corps.

In starting to organize the corps badges into some sequence that could be followed, we began by listing the corps in alphabetical order. To establish that order, the name of the corps in effect during World War II was used, the reasoning being that most collectors would easily recognize the familiar names of the World War II period. For example, 85 is the Royal Canadian Army Medical Corps and 145 is the Royal Canadian Field Artillery.

After assigning a number to the corps, we then assigned a second group of numbers to the battalions, companies or service units that comprise the main formation of the corps. For example, 85 denotes the Royal Canadian Army Medical Corps and 3 for the Canadian Stationary Hospitals, so the number now becomes 85-3 for the C.A.M.C. Stationary Hospitals. Another example is 145 for the Royal Canadian Field Artillery and then 145-3 for the C.F.A. Overseas Field Battery.

Now, within the main type of battalions, companies or service units that comprise a corps, we added a third group of numbers to indicate a specific battalion, company or service unit badge. The addition of A, B or C to this number indicates that the battalion, company or service unit badge has more than one design. For example, 85 denotes the Royal Canadian Army Medical Corps, 3 for the Canadian Stationary Hospitals and 8 for the 8th Canadian Stationary Hospital, so the number now become 85-3-8 for C.A.M.C. 8th Stationary Hospital.

Following the badge-variety number is a two-digit number relating to the different insignia. The numbers are broken down as follows:

01 - 19 OR's cap (glengarry)
20 - 39 Officers' cap badges
40 - 59 OR's collar badges
60 - 79 Officers' collar badges
80 - 90 OR's and NCO "C" over numeral collar badges
91 - 99 OR's shoulder numerals and titles

Within these groups the catalogue listings are jump numbered 02, 04, 06, etc. This system will allow for new findings which will undoubtedly occur. They then can be entered into the listings without disturbing the numbers already in place. The last group of numbers are identical to the system used to number the caps, collars and shoulder titles of the infantry battalions in *The Charlton Standard Catalogue of First World War Canadian Infantry Badges*.

CANADIAN ARMY VETERINARY CORPS

The Canadian Army Veterinary Corps was established in 1910 as a unit of the Non-Permanent Active Militia. Its primary task was the care of over thirty-one thousand horses. Within three weeks of the outbreak World War 1, two sections of the corps were attending to nine thousand horses in Canada, at the newly opened Camp Valcartier in Quebec. With the diminishing use of horses in warfare, the corps was disbanded shortly after the war.

No.: 5-1-1

GENERAL SERVICE BADGES

MAPLE LEAF DESIGN

CYPHER "CAV"

Makers: Gaunt
Fasteners: Lugs
Composition:
Other Ranks: Browning copper; blackened copper or brass
Officers: Sterling silver
Ref.: Babin 11-2, Cox 434

Badge No.	Insignia	Rank	Description	Extremely Fine
5-1-1-2	Cap	ORs	Browning copper; Gaunt	40.00
5-1-1-4		ORs	Blackened copper; Gaunt	65.00
5-1-1-6		ORs	Blackened brass; Gaunt	65.00
5-1-1-21		Officers	Sterling silver; Gaunt	150.00
5-1-1-41	Collars	ORs	Browning copper; Gaunt	18.00
5-1-1-43		ORs	Blackened copper	20.00
5-1-1-45		ORs	Blackened brass; Gaunt	18.00
5-1-1-61		Officers	Sterling silver; Gaunt	75.00
5-1-1-91	Shoulders	ORs	Title: "CAVC"	16.00

CANADIAN ARMY VETERINARY CORPS

No.: 5-1-3A

WREATH OF MAPLE LEAVES — OPEN

CYPHER "CVC"

Makers: Scully, Tiptaft, Unknown
Fasteners: Lugs
Composition:
  Other Ranks: Pickled brass; browning copper
  Officers:
    A: Gilt on silver
    B: Gilt with silver cypher
Ref.: Babin 11-2A, Cox 433

Note: Three varieties of this cap badge exist:
1. Tiptaft — plain letters, void field, beaver with head down
2. Unknown — framed letters, solid field
3. Scully — plain letters, void field, beaver with head up

Badge No.	Insignia	Rank	Description	Extremely Fine
5-1-3A-2	Cap	ORs	Pickled brass, void; Tiptaft	35.00
5-1-3A-4		ORs	Browning copper, solid; Unknown	50.00
5-1-3A-6		ORs	Browning copper, void; Scully	50.00
5-1-3A-21		Officers	Gilt on silver; Unknown	75.00
5-1-3A-23		Officers	Gilt with silver cypher; Unknown	75.00
5-1-3A-41	Collars	ORs	Pickled brass, void; Tiptaft	18.00
5-1-3A-43		ORs	Browning copper, solid; Unknown	20.00
5-1-3A-45		ORs	Browning copper, void; Scully	20.00
5-1-3A-61		Officers	Gilt on silver; Unknown	20.00
5-1-3A-63		Officers	Gilt with silver cypher; Unknown	40.00

No.: 5-1-3B

WREATH OF MAPLE LEAVES — CLOSED

CYPHER "CVC"

Makers: Unknown
Fasteners: Lugs
Composition:
   Other Ranks: Browning copper
   Officers: Unknown
Ref.: Babin 11-2B, Cox 432

Badge No.	Insignia	Rank	Description	Extremely Fine
5-1-3B-2	Cap	ORs	Browning copper; Unknown	50.00
5-1-3B-21		Officers	Unknown	- -
5-1-3B-41	Collars	ORs	Unknown	- -
5-1-3B-61		Officers	Unknown	- -

THE CANADIAN CAVALRY CORPS

1ST CANADIAN CAVALRY BRIGADE

The 1st Canadian Cavalry Brigade comprised the Royal Canadian Dragoons, Lord Strathcona's Horse and the Fort Garry Horse.

No.: 10-1-1 **ROYAL CANADIAN DRAGOONS**

The Royal Canadian Dragoons was mobilized in Valcartier, Quebec, and sailed overseas in September 1914, entering France as part of the 1st Canadian Division.

ROYAL CANADIAN DRAGOONS

Makers: Tiptaft, Unknown
Fasteners: Lugs
Composition:
Other Ranks: Pickled copper or brass; Browning brass
Officers: Gilt on brass
Ref.: Babin 10-2, Stewart, Cox 301

Badge No.	Insignia	Rank	Description	Extremely Fine
10-1-1-2	Cap	ORs	Pickled copper; Unknown	8.00
10-1-1-4		ORs	Pickled brass; Unknown	8.00
10-1-1-6		ORs	Browning brass; Tiptaft	8.00
10-1-1-21		Officers	Gilt on brass; Unknown	15.00
10-1-1-41	Collars	ORs	Pickled copper; Unknown	5.00
10-1-1-43		ORs	Pickled brass; Unknown	5.00
10-1-1-45		ORs	Browning brass; Tiptaft	5.00
10-1-1-61		Officers	Gilt on brass; Unknown	10.00
10-1-1-91	Shoulders	ORs	Title: "R.C.D."	5.00
10-1-1-93		ORs	Title: "111/DIVISIONAL CAVALRY/CANADA"	25.00

No.: 10-1-3   **LORD STRATHCONA'S HORSE
(ROYAL CANADIANS)**

Lord Strathcona's Horse entered France as part of the 1st Canadian Division, later becoming part of the 1st Canadian Cavalry Brigade.

*PERSEVERANCE/LORD STRATHCONA'S
HORSE ROYAL CANADIANS*

Makers: Tiptaft, Unknown
Fasteners: Lugs
Composition:
Other Ranks: Pickled copper; browning copper; blackened copper
Officers: Gilt on copper
Ref.: Babin 10-1, Stewart, Cox 302

Badge No.	Insignia	Rank	Description	Extremely Fine
10-1-3-2	Cap	ORs	Pickled brass; Unknown	20.00
10-1-3-4		ORs	Browning copper; Tiptaft	20.00
10-1-3-6		ORs	Blackened copper; Tiptaft	20.00
10-1-3-21		Officers	Gilt on copper, Tiptaft	75.00
10-1-3-41	Collars	ORs	Browning copper; Tiptaft	20.00
10-1-3-43		ORs	Blackened copper; Tiptaft	20.00
10-1-3-61		Officers	Gilt on copper; Tiptaft	30.00
10-1-3-91	Shoulders	ORs	Title: "STRATHCONA'S" in semi-circle	15.00
10-1-3-93		ORs	Title: "LSH"	10.00

6 • THE CANADIAN CAVALRY CORPS

No.: 10-1-5 **FORT GARRY HORSE**

Fort Garry Horse formed part of the 1st Canadian Division and later became part of the 1st Canadian Cavalry Brigade.

FACTA NON VERBA

Makers: Tiptaft
Fasteners: Lugs
Composition:
Other Ranks: Pickled brass; browning copper; blackened copper
Officers: Browning copper with Wm. overlay on design
Ref.: Babin 10-3, Stewart

Badge No.	Insignia	Rank	Description	Extremely Fine
		Maple Leaf Design		
10-1-5-2	Cap	ORs	Pickled brass	50.00
10-1-5-4		ORs	Browning copper	50.00
10-1-5-21		Officers	Browning copper, Wm overlay on design	175.00
		Fort Design		
10-1-5-6	Cap	ORs	Pickled brass	--
		Maple Leaf Design		
10-1-5-41	Collars	ORs	Pickled brass	10.00
10-1-5-43		ORs	Browning copper	10.00
10-1-5-61		Officers	Browning copper, Wm overlay on design	75.00
		Fort Design		
10-1-5-45	Collars	ORs	Pickled brass	15.00
10-1-5-47		ORs	Blackened copper	--
10-1-5-49		ORs	Browning copper	15.00
10-1-5-63		Officers	Browning copper, Wm overlay on design	25.00
10-1-5-91	Shoulders	ORs	Title: "F.G.H."	15.00
10-1-5-93		ORs	Title: "F.G.H." over "CANADA"	20.00

2ND CANADIAN CAVALRY BRIGADE

No.: 10-3-1

MOUNTED RIFLE BRIGADE

2/MOUNTED RIFLES BRIGADE/CANADA

Makers: Inglis
Fasteners: Lugs
Composition:
  Other Ranks: Pickled copper
  Officers: Unknown
Ref.: Babin, Stewart, Cox 328

Badge No.	Insignia	Rank	Description	Extremely Fine
10-3-1-2	Cap	ORs	Pickled copper; Inglis	50.00
10-3-1-21		Officers	Unknown	- -
10-3-1-41	Collars	ORs	Pickled copper; Inglis	Rare
10-3-1-61		Officers	Unknown	- -
10-3-1-91	Shoulders	ORs	Unknown	- -

THE CANADIAN LIGHT HORSE

The Canadian Light Horse regiment was formed by volunteers from the Royal North West Mounted Police, the 1st Hussars, the 16th Canadian Light Horse, and the 19th Alberta Dragoons, with each unit wearing its own badges.

No.: 10-5-1   ROYAL NORTH WEST MOUNTED POLICE

CANADA/MAINTIEN LE DROIT/ROYAL NORTH WEST MOUNTED POLICE

Makers: Gaunt, Scully
Fasteners: Lugs
Composition:
Other Ranks: Pickled copper; browning copper or brass
Officers: Gilt on brass
Ref.: Babin 10-7, Stewart, Cox 304

Note: Two makers of this cap badge exist:
1. Gaunt: — framed ribbons
2. Scully: — plain ribbons

Badge No.	Insignia	Rank	Description	Extremely Fine
10-5-1-2	Cap	ORs	Pickled copper; Gaunt	--
10-5-1-4		ORs	Browning copper; Scully	200.00
10-5-1-6		ORs	Browning brass; Gaunt	200.00
10-5-1-21		Officers	Gilt on brass; Gaunt	350.00
10-5-1-41	Collars	ORs	Pickled copper; Gaunt	--
10-5-1-43		ORs	Browning copper; Scully	65.00
10-5-1-45		ORs	Browning brass; Gaunt	65.00
10-5-1-61		Officers	Gilt on brass; Gaunt	100.00
10-5-1-91	Shoulders	ORs	Title: "RNWMP;" Scully	50.00
10-5-1-93		ORs	Title: "RNWMP;" Gaunt	50.00

No.: 10-5-3

1ST HUSSARS

FIRST HUSSARS/HODIE NON CRAS/CANADA

Makers: Scully, Tiptaft
Fasteners: Lugs
Composition:
  Other Ranks: Browning brass
  Officers: Gilt on brass
Ref.: Babin 10-4, Stewart

Badge No.	Insignia	Rank	Description	Extremely Fine
10-5-3-2	Cap	ORs	Browning brass; Scully	25.00
10-5-3-4		ORs	Browning brass; Tiptaft	25.00
10-5-3-21		Officers	Gilt on brass; Scully	75.00
10-5-3-41	Collars	ORs	Browning brass	15.00
10-5-3-61		Officers	Gilt on brass; Scully	25.00
10-5-3-91	Shoulders	ORs	Title: "HUSSARS"	15.00

No.: 10-5-5

19TH ALBERTA DRAGOONS

ALBERTA 19 DRAGOONS

Makers: Gaunt, Scully
Fasteners: Lugs
Composition:
Other Ranks: Browning brass
Officers: Gilt brass with silver ribbon
Ref.: Babin 10-6, Cox 307 (cap), 308 (collar)

Badge No.	Insignia	Rank	Description	Extremely Fine
10-5-5-2	Cap	ORs	Browning brass; Scully	40.00
10-5-5-4		ORs	Browning brass; Gaunt	40.00
10-5-5-21		Officers	Gilt brass, silver ribbon; Gaunt	200.00
10-5-5-41	Collars	ORs	Browning brass; Scully	35.00
10-5-5-43		ORs	Browning brass; Gaunt	35.00
10-5-5-61		Officers	Gilt brass, silver ribbon; Gaunt	75.00
10-5-5-91	Shoulders	ORs	Title: "XIX DRAGOONS"	35.00

16TH CANADIAN LIGHT HORSE

FOR KING AND EMPIRE

No.: 10-5-7

Makers: Scully, Tiptaft
Fasteners: Lugs
Composition:
 Other Ranks: Browning copper or brass
 Officers:
  A: Bronze with silver overlay on design
  B: Gilt on copper
Ref.: Babin 10-5, Stewart, Cox 305 and 306

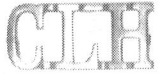

Badge No.	Insignia	Rank	Description	Extremely Fine
10-5-7-2	Cap	ORs	Browning copper; Scully	50.00
10-5-7-4		ORs	Browning brass; Tiptaft	25.00
10-5-7-21		Officers	Bronze, silver overlay on design	150.00
10-5-7-23		Officers	Gilt on copper	150.00
10-5-7-41	Collars	ORs	Browning copper; Scully	20.00
10-5-7-43		ORs	Browning brass; Tiptaft	20.00
10-5-7-61		Officers	Bronze, silver overlay on design	25.00
10-5-7-63		Officers	Gilt on copper	50.00
10-5-7-91	Shoulders	ORs	Title: "CLH"	10.00

CANADIAN MOUNTED RIFLE BATTALIONS

No.: 10-7-1 **1ST MOUNTED RIFLE BATTALION**

The 1st Mounted Rifle Battalion was organized on March 15, 1915, in Brandon, Manitoba. It served in France from September 21, 1915, until the armistice and disbanded on November 15, 1920.

**FIRST MOUNTED RIFLES/
MANITOBA CANADA SASKATCHEWAN**

Makers: Dingwall, Ellis, Scully, Tiptaft
Fasteners: Lugs, slide
Composition:
Other Ranks: Browning copper or brass
Officers: Sterling silver
Ref.: Babin 4-1, Stewart, Cox 309

Badge No.	Insignia	Rank	Description	Extremely Fine
10-7-1-2	Cap	ORs	Browning copper; Dingwall	15.00
10-7-1-4		ORs	Browning brass; Tiptaft	20.00
10-7-1--21		Officers	Sterling silver; Dingwall	150.00
10-7-1-41	Collars	ORs	Browning copper; Dingwall	25.00
10-7-1-43		ORs	Browning brass; Tiptaft	30.00
10-7-1-61		Officers	Sterling silver; Dingwall	50.00
10-7-1-91	Shoulders	ORs	Letters "M.R.;" Ellis	10.00
10-7-1-93		ORs	Letters "M.R.;" Scully	10.00
10-7-1-95		ORs	Title: "FIRST MOUNTED RIFLES CANADA;" Tiptaft	30.00
10-7-1-97		ORs	Title: "CMR;" Plain; Ellis	10.00
10-7-1-99		ORs	Title: "CMR;" Serifs; Tiptaft	10.00
10-7-1-101		ORs	Title: "CMR OVER CANADA"	20.00

THE CANADIAN CAVALRY CORPS • 13

No.: 10-7-2 **2ND MOUNTED RIFLE BATTALION**

Organized in Victoria, B.C., on March 15, 1915, the 2nd Mounted Rifle Battalion began serving in France in September 1915. It was disbanded on November 15, 1920.

WITH BRACKETS AROUND "B.C.H."

No. - 10-7-2A *2ND C.M.R. (B.C.H.) CANADA*

Makers: Jacoby, Tiptaft, Unknown
Fasteners: Lugs, slide
Composition:
 Other Ranks: Browning copper
 Officers: Unknown
Ref.: Babin, Stewart,
Cox 310 (collar), 311 (cap)

Note: Two makers of this cap badge exist:
 1. Jacoby — plain ribbons
 2. Tiptaft — framed ribbons

Badge No.	Insignia	Rank	Description	Extremely Fine
10-7-2A-2	Cap	ORs	Browning copper; Jacoby	18.00
10-7-2A-4		ORs	Browning copper; Tiptaft	18.00
10-7-2A-21		Officers		Unknown - -
10-7-2A-4	Collars	ORs	Browning copper; Jacoby	14.00
10-7-2A-43		ORs	Browning copper; Tiptaft	14.00
10-7-2A-61		Officers	Unknown	- -
10-7-2A-9	Shoulders	ORs	Title: "2nd C.M.R. (B.C. Horse) Canada;" Jacoby	25.00
10-7-2A-93		ORs	Title "2nd C.M.R. (B.C. Horse) Canada;" Tiptaft	25.00

14 • THE CANADIAN CAVALRY CORPS

No. - 10-7-2B **WITHOUT BRACKETS AROUND "B.C.H."**

2ND C.M.R. B.C.H. CANADA

Makers: Tiptaft, Unknown
Fasteners: Lugs
Composition:
Other Ranks: Gilt on copper
   Officers: Unknown
Ref.: Not previously listed

Badge No.	Insignia	Rank	Description	Extremely Fine
10-7-2B-2	Cap	ORs	Gilt on copper; Tiptaft	200.00
10-7-2B-21		Officers	Unknown	- -
10-7-2B-41	Collars	ORs	Unknown	- -
10-7-2B-61		Officers	Unknown	- -

No.: 10-7-3   **3RD MOUNTED RIFLE BATTALION**

The 3rd Mounted Rifle Battalion was organized in Medicine Hat, Alberta, on March 15, 1915. It served in France and Holland during World War 1 and was disbanded on November 15, 1920.

3/MOUNTED RIFLES CANADA

Makers: Jacoby, Unknown
Fasteners: Lugs, tangs
Composition:
  Other Ranks: Browning copper or brass
  Officers: Unknown
Ref.: Babin 4-3, Stewart, Cox 312 (cap), 313 (collar)

Badge No.	Insignia	Rank	Description	Extremely Fine
10-7-3-2	Cap	ORs	Browning copper; Jacoby	15.00
10-7-3-4		ORs	Browning brass; Jacoby	25.00
10-7-3-21		Officers	Unknown	- -
10-7-3-41	Collars	ORs	Browning brass	20.00
10-7-3-61		Officers	Unknown	- -

No.: 10-7-4 4TH MOUNTED RIFLE BATTALION

The 4th Mounted Rifle Battalion was organized on March 15, 1915, in Toronto, Ontario. It served in France and Holland and was disbanded on November 15, 1920.

No. - 10-7-4A 4/C.M.R./OVERSEAS

Makers: Ellis, Tiptaft
Fasteners: Lugs
Composition:
Other Ranks: Browning brass or copper
Officers: Unknown
Ref.: Babin 4-4

Note: Two makers of this cap exist:
 1. Ellis — plain ribbon
 2. Tiptaft — framed ribbon

Badge No.	Insignia	Rank	Description	Extremely Fine
10-7-4A-2	Cap	ORs	Browning copper; Tiptaft	50.00
10-7-4A-4		ORs	Browning brass; Ellis	50.00
10-7-4A-21		Officers	Unknown	- -
10-7-4A-41	Collars	ORs	Browning copper; Tiptaft	65.00
10-7-4A-43		ORs	Browning brass; Ellis	65.00
10-7-4A-61		Officers	Unknown	- -

THE CANADIAN CAVALRY CORPS • 17

No. - 10-7-4B   *4/C.M.R.R./OVERSEAS*

Makers: Tiptaft, Unknown
Fasteners: Lugs, slide
Composition:
 Other Ranks: Browning copper or brass
 Officers: Unknown
Ref.: Babin 4-4A, Cox 314

Note: Three makers of this cap badge exist:
 1. Tiptaft — plain ribbons, curved left horn with nine points
 2. Tiptaft — plain ribbons, curved left horn with six points
 3. Unknown 1 — framed ribbons, straight left horn with three points

Badge No.	Insignia	Rank	Description	Extremely Fine
10-7-4B-2	Cap	ORs	Browning copper; Unknown 1	60.00
10-7-4B-4		ORs	Browning copper; Tiptaft	25.00
10-7-4B-6		ORs	Browning copper; Unknown 2	25.00
10-7-4B-8		ORs	Browning brass; Tiptaft	25.00
10-7-4B-21		Officers	Unknown	--
10-7-4B-41	Collars	ORs	Browning copper; Unknown 1	16.00
10-7-4B-43		ORs	Browning copper; Tiptaft	16.00
10-7-4B-45		ORs	Browning copper; Unknown 2	16.00
10-7-4B-47		ORs	Browning brass; Tiptaft	16.00
10-7-4B-61		Officers	Unknown	--
10-7-4B-91	Shoulders	ORs	Title: "C.M.R.R."	25.00

18 • THE CANADIAN CAVALRY CORPS

No.: 10-7-5   **5TH MOUNTED RIFLE BATTALION**

Organized in Sherbrooke, Quebec, on March 15, 1915, the 5th Mounted Rifle Battalion served in France and Holland. It was disbanded on November 15, 1920.

OVERSEAS/MOUNTED 5TH RIFLES/CANADA

Makers: Gaunt, Inglis, Tiptaft
Fasteners: Lugs
Composition:
Other Ranks: Pickled copper or brass; browning copper
Officers: Unknown
Ref.: Babin 4-5, Stewart, Cox 315

Note: Three makers of this cap badge exist:
1. Inglis *(Illustrated)* — pointed leaf design, plain ribbons
2. Tiptaft — blunt leaf design, framed ribbons
3. Gaunt — blunt leaf design, plain ribbons

Badge No.	Insignia	Rank	Description	Extremely Fine
10-7-5-2	Cap	ORs	Pickled copper; Inglis	20.00
10-7-5-4		ORs	Pickled copper; Tiptaft	25.00
10-7-5-6		ORs	Pickled brass; Gaunt	25.00
10-7-5-8		ORs	Browning copper; Gaunt	25.00
10-7-5-21		Officers	Unknown	--
10-7-5-41	Collars	ORs	Pickled copper; Inglis	20.00
10-7-5-43		ORs	Pickled copper; Tiptaft	20.00
10-7-5-45		ORs	Pickled brass; Gaunt	15.00
10-7-5-47		ORs	Browning copper; Gaunt	20.00
10-7-5-61		Officers	Unknown	--
10-7-5-91	Shoulders	ORs	Title: "5/CMR/CANADA"	25.00

THE CANADIAN CAVALRY CORPS • 19

No.: 10-7-6   **6TH MOUNTED RIFLE BATTALION**

The 6th Mounted Rifle Battalion was organized on March 15, 1915, in Amherst, Nova Scotia. It was disbanded on November 15, 1920.

6/OVERSEAS/MOUNTED RIFLES/CANADA

Makers: Inglis, Tiptaft
Fasteners: Lugs
Composition:
Other Ranks: Pickled copper or brass; browning copper or brass
Officers: Unknown
Ref.: Babin 4-6, Stewart, Cox 316 (cap), 317 (collar)

Note: Two makers of this cap badge exist:
1. Inglis — pointed leaf design, plain ribbons
2. Tiptaft — blunt leaf design, framed ribbons
The Inglis collars are facing (right and left), while the Tiptaft collars are not.

Badge No.	Insignia	Rank	Description	Extremely Fine
10-7-6-2	Cap	ORs	Pickled copper; Inglis	30.00
10-7-6-4		ORs	Pickled brass; Inglis	30.00
10-7-6-6		ORs	Pickled brass; Tiptaft	20.00
10-7-6-8		ORs	Browning copper; Tiptaft	30.00
10-7-6-10		ORs	Browning brass; Tiptaft	20.00
10-7-6-21		Officers	Unknown	- -
10-7-6-41	Collars	ORs	Pickled copper; Inglis	20.00
10-7-6-43		ORs	Pickled brass; Inglis	20.00
10-7-6-45		ORs	Pickled brass; Tiptaft	20.00
10-7-6-47		ORs	Browning copper	20.00
10-7-6-49		ORs	Browning brass	20.00
10-7-6-61		Officers	Unknown	- -

No.: 10-7-7   7TH MOUNTED RIFLE BATTALION

Organized in London, Ontario, on March 15, 1915, the 7th Mounted Rifle Battalion formed the Canadian Mounted Rifle Depot in England. The "A" Squadron reorganized as the 2nd Divisional Cavalry Squadron.

CANADA

Makers: As general list
Fasteners: Lugs
Composition:
Other Ranks: As general list
Officers: As general list
Ref.: Babin 4-7, Stewart, Cox 318

Badge No.	Insignia	Rank	Description	Extremely Fine
10-7-7-2	Cap	ORs	General list	10.00
10-7-7-21		Officers	General list	15.00
10-7-7-41	Collars	ORs	General list	10.00
10-7-7-61		Officers	General list	15.00
10-7-7-91	Shoulders	ORs	Title: "7 CMR"	150.00

THE CANADIAN CAVALRY CORPS • 21

No.: 10-7-8 **8TH MOUNTED RIFLE BATTALION**

This battalion was organized in Ottawa, Ontario, on March 15, 1915. It was broken up to provide reinforcements and was finally disbanded on November 15, 1920.

8/CANADIAN MOUNTED RIFLES

Makers: Birks, Tiptaft
Fasteners: Lugs
Composition:
  Other Ranks: Browning copper or brass
  Officers: Gilt on copper
Ref.: Babin 4-8, Stewart, Cox 319

Note: Two makers of this cap badge exist:
  1. Birks *(cap illustrated)* — plain ribbons
  2. Tiptaft *(collars illustrated)* — framed ribbons

Badge No.	Insignia	Rank	Description	Extremely Fine
10-7-8-2	Cap	ORs	Browning copper; Birks	20.00
10-7-8-4		ORs	Browning copper; Tiptaft	30.00
10-7-8-6		ORs	Browning brass; Tiptaft	30.00
10-7-8-21		Officers	Gilt on copper	75.00
10-7-8-41	Collars	ORs	Browning copper; Birks	20.00
10-7-8-43		ORs	Browning copper; Tiptaft	20.00
10-7-8-45		ORs	Browning brass; Tiptaft	12.00
10-7-8-61		Officers	Gilt on copper	25.00
10-7-8-91	Shoulders	ORs	Title: "8/CMR"	20.00
10-7-8-93		Officers	Gilt on copper	30.00

No.: 10-7-9   9TH MOUNTED RIFLE BATTALION

The 9th Mounted Rifle Battalion was organized on March 15, 1915, in Lloydminster, Saskatchewan. It was broken up to provide reinforcements, and was finally disbanded on November 15, 1920.

OVERSEAS MOUNTED RIFLES/9/CANADA

Makers: Hemsley, Inglis, Tiptaft, Unknown
Fasteners: Lugs, tangs
Composition:
  Other Ranks: Pickled copper or brass; browning copper
  Officers: Unknown
Ref.: Babin 4-9, Stewart, Cox 320 (cap), 321 (collars)

Note: Three varieties of this cap badge exist:
  1. Hemsley, Inglis — pointed leaf design, wide nine, plain ribbons
  2. Unknown *(illustrated)* — blunt leaf design, plain ribbons
  3. Tiptaft — blunt leaf design, narrow nine, framed Canada ribbon

Badge No.	Insignia	Rank	Description	Extremely Fine
10-7-9-2	Cap	ORs	Pickled copper; Hemsley, Inglis	25.00
10-7-9-4		ORs	Pickled brass; Unknown	25.00
10-7-9-6		ORs	Pickled brass; Tiptaft	25.00
10-7-9-8		ORs	Browning copper; Hemsley, Inglis	25.00
10-7-9-10		ORs	Browning copper; Unknown	25.00
10-7-9-21		Officers	Unknown	- -
10-7-9-41	Collars	ORs	Pickled copper; Hemsley, Inglis	18.00
10-7-9-43		ORs	Pickled brass; Unknown	20.00
10-7-9-45		ORs	Pickled brass; Tiptaft	20.00
10-7-9-47		ORs	Browning copper; Hemsley, Inglis	18.00
10-7-9-49		ORs	Browning copper; Unknown	18.00
10-7-9-61		Officers	Unknown	- -
10-7-9-91	Shoulders	ORs	Title: "9TH M.R. CANADA:" Hemsley, Inglis	30.00

THE CANADIAN CAVALRY CORPS • 23

No.: 10-7-10   **10TH MOUNTED RIFLE BATTALION**

The 10th Mounted Rifle Battalion was organized on March 15, 1915, in Portage La Prairie, Manitoba. It was broken up to provide reinforcements for other units. The battalion was disbanded on November 15th, 1920.

FOR KING & EMPIRE OVERSEAS/X/CANADIAN MOUNTED RIFLES

Makers: Dingwall, Tiptaft
Fasteners: Lugs, slide, tangs
Composition:
 Other Ranks: Browning copper
 Officers: Pickled copper
Ref.: Babin 4-10, Stewart, Cox 322 (cap), 323 (collar)

Note: Two makers of this cap badge exist:
 1. Dingwall — pointed leaf design, plain ribbons
 2. Tiptaft — blunt leaf design, framed ribbons

Badge No.	Insignia	Rank	Description	Extremely Fine
10-7-10-2	Cap	ORs	Browning copper; Dingwall	20.00
10-7-10-4		ORs	Browning copper; Tiptaft	20.00
10-7-10-21		Officers	Pickled copper, flat back; Dingwall	25.00
10-7-10-41	Collars	ORs	Browning copper; Dingwall	20.00
10-7-10-43		ORs	Browning copper; Tiptaft	20.00
10-7-10-61		Officers	Pickled copper, flat back; Dingwall	20.00
10-7-10-91	Shoulders	ORs	Title: "10" over "Mounted Rifles," small oval "o" in "Mounted;" Inglis	25.00
10-7-10-93		ORs	Title: "10" over "Mounted Rifles", large oval "o" in "Mounted;" Tiptaft	25.00

No.: 10-7-11   11TH MOUNTED RIFLE BATTALION

This battalion was organized on March 15, 1915, in Vancouver, British Columbia. It was broken up to provide reinforcements for other units and was disbanded on November 15th, 1920.

C.M.R./11/CANADA

Makers: Jacoby
Fasteners: Lugs, pin
Composiotion:
  Other Ranks: Browning copper; blackened copper
  Officers:
    A: Sterling silver
    B: Gilt on brass
Ref.: Babin 4-11, Stewart, Cox 324

Style One   Style Two

Note: Two styles of this cap badge exist, both by Jacoby:
1. Jacoby, style one — domed leaf design, plain ribbons
2. Jacoby, style two — blunt leaf design, framed ribbon

Badge No.	Insignia	Rank	Description	Extremely Fine
10-7-11-2	Cap	ORs	Browning copper; Jacoby	25.00
10-7-11-4		ORs	Browning copper; Jacoby	25.00
10-7-11-6		ORs	Blackened copper; Jacoby	25.00
10-7-11-21		Officers	Sterling silver; Jacoby	75.00
10-7-11-23		Officers	Gilt on brass; Jacoby	75.00
10-7-11-41	Collars	ORs	Browning copper; Jacoby	16.00
10-7-11-43		ORs	Browning copper; Jacoby	16.00
10-7-11-45		ORs	Blackened copper; Jacoby	16.00
10-7-11-61		Officers	Sterling silver; Jacoby	30.00
10-7-11-63		Officers	Gilt on brass; Jacoby	50.00
10-7-11-91	Shoulders	ORs	Title: "11th C.M.R. CANADA," brass; Jacoby	20.00
10-7-11-93		Officers	Title: "11th C.M.R. CANADA," silver; Jacoby	35.00

12TH MOUNTED RIFLE BATTALION

No.: 10-7-12

The 12th Mounted Rifle Battalion was organized on March 15, 1915, at Calgary, Alberta. It was broken up to provide reinforcements for other units in the field. The battalion was disbanded on November 15, 1920.

OVERSEAS/12/MOUNTED RIFLES/CANADA

Makers: Hemsley, Inglis, Tiptaft
Fasteners: Lugs
Composition:
Other Ranks: Browning copper or brass
Officers: Unknown
Ref.: Babin 4-12, Stewart, Cox 325

Note: Two makers of this cap badge exist:
1. Hemsley, Inglis *(illustrated)* — pointed leaf design, pointed serif on 2
2. Tiptaft — blunt leaf design, blunt serif on 2

Badge No.	Insignia	Rank	Description	Extremely Fine
10-7-12-2	Cap	ORs	Browning copper; Hemsley, Inglis	20.00
10-7-12-4		ORs	Browning brass; Tiptaft	20.00
10-7-12-21		Officers	Unknown	- -
10-7-12-41	Collars	ORs	Browning copper; Hemsley, Inglis	15.00
10-7-12-43		ORs	Browning brass; Tiptaft	15.00
10-7-12-61		Officers	Unknown	- -
10-7-12-91	Shoulders	ORs	Title: "12/CMR/CANADA;" Unknown	20.00

No.: 10-7-13   13TH MOUNTED RIFLE BATTALION

The 13th Mounted Rifle Battalion was organized on March 15, 1915, in Medicine Hat, Alberta. It was broken up to provide reinforcements for other units in the field. The battalion was disbanded on November 15, 1920.

OVERSEAS/13/MOUNTED RIFLES/CANADA

Makers: Hemsley, Inglis, Service Supply
Fasteners: Lugs
Composition:
  Other Ranks: Pickled brass; browning copper
  Officers: Unknown
Ref.: Babin 4-13, Stewart, Cox 326

Note: Two makers of this cap badge exist:
  1. Hemsley, Inglis *(illustrated)* — pointed leaf design, plain ribbon
  2. Service Supply — blunt leaf design, framed legends

Badge No.	Insignia	Rank	Description	Extremely Fine
10-7-13-2	Cap	ORs	Pickled brass; Hemsley, Inglis	35.00
10-7-13-4		ORs	Browning copper; Service Supply	35.00
10-7-13-21		Officers	Unknown	--
10-7-13-41	Collars	ORs	Pickled brass; Hemsley, Inglis	22.00
10-7-13-43		ORs	Browning copper; Service Supply	22.00
10-7-13-61		Officers	Unknown	--
10-7-13-91	Shoulders	ORs	Title: "13 C.M.R."	30.00

No.: 10-9-1

CANADIAN MOUNTED RIFLE DRAFT

CANADA/MOUNTED RIFLES/OVERSEAS

Makers: Ellis, Tiptaft
Fasteners: Pins, lugs
Composition:
Other Ranks: Pickled copper or brass; blackened brass
Officers:
  A: Gilt on brass with enamelled overlay on design
  B: Sterling silver
Ref.: Babin 4-14, Stewart, Cox 327

Note: Two makers of this cap badge exist:
  1. Ellis — pointed, smooth leaf design, plain ribbons
  2. Tiptaft *(illustrated)* — blunt, pebbled leaf design, framed ribbons

Badge No.	Insignia	Rank	Description	Extremely Fine
10-9-1-2	Cap	ORs	Pickled copper; Ellis	75.00
10-9-1-4		ORs	Pickled brass; Ellis	75.00
10-9-1-6		ORs	Blackened brass; Tiptaft	85.00
10-9-1-21		Officers	Gilt on brass, enamelled overlay on design; Ellis	175.00
10-9-1-23		Officers	Sterling silver; Ellis	150.00
10-9-1-41	Collars	ORs	Pickled copper; Ellis	20.00
10-9-1-43		ORs	Pickled brass; Ellis	20.00
10-9-1-45		ORs	Blackened brass; Tiptaft	20.00
10-9-1-61		Officers	Gilt on brass, enamelled overlay on design; Ellis	50.00
10-9-1-63		Officers	Sterling silver	25.00
10-9-1-91	Shoulders	ORs	Title: "C.M.R."	10.00

CANADIAN CORPS

No.: 15-1-1   **CANADIAN MILITARY HEADQUARTERS**

CANADIAN MILITARY H.Q.

Makers: Unknown
Fasteners: Lugs
Composition:
 Other Ranks: Unknown
    Officers: Sterling silver
Ref.: Cox 937

Badge No.	Insignia	Rank	Description	Extremely Fine
15-1-1-2	Cap	ORs	Unknown	- -
15-1-1-21		Officers	Sterling silver	250.00
15-1-1-41	Collars	ORs	Unknown	- -
15-1-1-61		Officers	Sterling silver	100.00
15-1-1-91	Shoulders	ORs	Unknown	- -

No.: 15-3-1   CORPS OF MILITARY STAFF CLERKS

Already part of the active militia at the outbreak of the Great War, the Corps of Military Staff Clerks held responsibility for all clerical duties and printing of field orders at the G.H.Q. staff level.

CORPS OF MILITARY STAFF CLERKS

Makers: Ellis, Roden
Fasteners: Lugs
Composition:
  Other Ranks: Copper; brass
  Officers: Unknown
Ref.: Babin 39-3, Stewart, Cox 940

Note: Two makers of this cap badge exist:
  1. Roden — solid
  2. Ellis *(illustrated)* — void

Badge No.	Insignia	Rank	Description	Extremely Fine
15-3-1-2	Cap	ORs	Copper, solid; Roden	50.00
15-3-1-4		ORs	Copper, void; Ellis	50.00
15-3-1-6		ORs	Brass, void; Ellis	50.00
15-3-1-21		Officers	Unknown	- -
15-3-1-41	Collars	ORs	Copper; Roden	25.00
15-3-1-43		ORs	Copper; Ellis	25.00
15-3-1-61		Officers	Unknown	- -
15-3-1-91	Shoulders	ORs	Title: "CMSC"	20.00

No.: 15-5-1   **DEPARTMENT OF THE GENERAL AUDITOR**

DEPT. OF THE GENERAL AUDITOR/C.E.F.

Makers: Gaunt
Fasteners: Lugs
Composition:
 Other Ranks: Browning copper with silver overlay on beaver
 Officers: Unknown
Ref.: Babin 39-13, Cox 941

Badge No.	Insignia	Rank	Description	Extremely Fine
15-5-1-2	Cap	ORs	Browning copper, silver overlay on beaver; Gaunt	300.00
15-5-1-21		Officers	Unknown	- -
15-5-1-41	Collars	ORs	Browning copper, silver overlay on beaver; Gaunt	100.00
15-5-1-61		Officers	Unknown	- -

INSTRUCTIONAL TROOPS

Instrumental in the advanced training of both the infantry and the cavalry, this unit comprised expert riflemen from the Canadian School of Musketry and the Cavalry School Corps.

No.: 15-7-1 **CANADIAN SCHOOL OF MUSKETRY**
WREATH OF MAPLE LEAVES DESIGN
WITH CYPHER "CSM"

Makers: Scully, Unknown
Fasteners: Lugs
Composition:
Other Ranks: Browning copper; blackened copper
Officers:
    A: Gilt on copper
    B: Unknown
Ref.: Babin 39-2, Cox 948

Note: Two makers of this cap badge exist:
    1. Caps 27 mm
    2. Caps 37 mm

Badge No.	Insignia	Rank	Description	Extremely Fine
15-7-1-2	Cap	ORs	Browning copper; Scully	50.00
15-7-1-4		ORs	Blackened copper; Unknown	50.00
15-7-1-21		Officers	Gilt on copper; Unknown	150.00
15-7-1-41	Collars	ORs	Browning copper; Scully	15.00
15-7-1-43		ORs	Blackened copper; Unknown	15.00
15-7-1-61		Officers	Gilt on copper; Unknown	30.00
15-7-1-63		Officers	Unknown	--
15-7-1-91	Shoulders	ORs	Title: "Musketry;" Scully	20.00

CANADIAN CORPS

No.: 15-7-3   **CANADIAN PHYSICAL INSTRUCTORS**

CANADA

Makers: Tiptaft, Unknown
Fasteners: Lugs
Composition:
  Other Ranks: Browning copper
       Officers: Unknown
Ref.: Babin 39-1, Cox 945 and 946

Large

Small

Note: Two types of this cap badge exist:
  1. Large — 5.7 mm x 5 mm, curved Canada ribbon
  2. Small — 4.8 mm x 4.7 mm, straight Canada ribbon

Badge No.	Insignia	Rank	Description	Extremely Fine
15-7-3-2	Cap	ORs	Browning copper, straight ribbon, large	30.00
15-7-3-4		ORs	Browning copper, curved ribbon, small	30.00
15-7-3-6		ORs	Browning copper, straight ribbon; Tiptaft	30.00
15-7-3-21		Officers	Unknown	- -
15-7-3-41	Collars	ORs	Browning copper, straight ribbon; Unknown	15.00
15-7-3-43		ORs	Browning copper, curved ribbon; Tiptaft	15.00
15-7-3-61		Officers	Unknown	- -
15-7-3-91	Shoulders	ORs	Unknown	- -

CANADIAN CORPS CYCLISTS • 33

CANADIAN CORPS CYCLISTS

The First Canadian Cyclist Company sailed for England with the 1st Canadian Division on October 14, 1914. Since it had been established that all further divisions must carry a cyclist battalion, recruiting was carried out by the Corps of Guides of the Non-Permanent Active Militia. In addition to their training in Canada, the Canadian Corps Cyclists began an intensive course in England, consisting of musketry, bombing, bayonet fighting, signalling, topography, range-finding and learning to use the Lewis guns. Almost one quarter of the men in the cyclists were killed during the war.

No.: 20-1-1   **GENERAL SERVICE BADGE**

CANADIAN/CORPS/CYCLIST BN.

Makers: Gaunt, Tiptaft
Fasteners: Lugs
Composition:
  Other Ranks: Browning brass
  Officers: Gilt on brass
Ref.: Babin 25-1. Cox 854

Note: Two makers of this cap badge exist:
  1. Tiptaft
  2. Gaunt

Badge No.	Insignia	Rank	Description	Extremely Fine
20-1-1-2	Cap	ORs	Browning brass; Tiptaft	25.00
20-1-1-4		ORs	Browning brass; Gaunt	25.00
20-1-1-21		Officers	Gilt on brass; Tiptaft	150.00
20-1-1-41	Collars	ORs	Browning brass; Tiptaft	20.00
20-1-1-43		ORs	Browning brass; Gaunt	20.00
20-1-1-61		Officers	Gilt on brass; Tiptaft	75.00
20-1-1-91	Shoulders	ORs	Title: "CYCLISTS" (Straight)	20.00
20-1-1-93		ORs	Title: "CYCLIST" (Straight)	20.00
20-1-1-95		ORs	Title: "CYCLIST" (Curved)	20.00
20-1-1-97		ORs	Title: "CYCLISTS/CANADA"	20.00

DIVISIONAL CYCLIST COMPANIES

No.: 20-3-1   **1ST DIVISIONAL CYCLIST COMPANY**

The 1st Divisional Cyclist Company was organized on August 6, 1914, and it was disbanded on November 15, 1920.

DIVISIONAL/CYCLISTS/OVERSEAS/CANADA

Makers: Roden Bros. (1917)
Fasteners: Lugs
Composition:
 Other Ranks: Pickled brass
  Officers: Unknown
Ref.: Babin 25-3, Cox 855

Badge No.	Insignia	Rank	Description	Extremely Fine
20-3-1-2	Cap	ORs	Pickled brass; Roden	25.00
20-3-1-21		Officers	Unknown	- -
20-3-1-41	Collars	ORs	Pickled brass; Roden	12.00
20-3-1-61		Officers	Unknown	- -

CANADIAN CORPS CYCLISTS • 35

No.: 20-3-2   **2ND DIVISIONAL CYCLIST COMPANY**

The 2nd Divisional Cyclist Company was organized in February 1915, and authorized April 6, 1915. It was disbanded on November 15, 1920.

No. - 20-3-2A   **WHEEL DESIGN**

DIVISIONAL CYCLISTS/2/CANADA

AUTHORIZED APRIL 6, 1915

Makers: F.T. Proctor, Tiptaft
Fasteners: Lugs, slide
Composition:
   Other Ranks: Browning copper or brass
   Officers: Gilt on brass
Ref.: Babin 25-4, Cox 851

Note: Two makers of this cap badge exist:
   1. Tiptaft — wide 2
   2. F. T. Proctor, Toronto *(illustrated)* — narrow 2

Badge No.	Insignia	Rank	Description	Extremely Fine
20-3-2A-2	Cap	ORs	Browning copper; Proctor	30.00
20-3-2A-4		ORs	Browning brass; Tiptaft	20.00
20-3-2A-21		Officers	Gilt on brass; Tiptaft	75.00
20-3-2A-41	Collars	ORs	Browning copper; Proctor	12.00
20-3-2A-43		ORs	Browning brass; Tiptaft	10.00
20-3-2A-61		Officers	Gilt on brass; Tiptaft	50.00

36 • CANADIAN CORPS CYCLISTS

No. - 20-3-2B**MAPLE LEAF DESIGN**

DIVISIONAL CYCLISTS/2/CANADA

Makers: Unknown
Fasteners: Lugs
Composition:
 Other Ranks: Browning copper
Officers: Unknown
Ref.: Not previously listed

Note: A collar badge is overlaid on a maple leaf.

Badge No.	Insignia	Rank	Description	Extremely Fine
20-3-2B-2	Cap	ORs	Browning copper	25.00
20-3-2B-21		Officers	Unknown	- -
20-3-2B-41	Collars	ORs	Browning copper	15.00
20-3-2B-61		Officers	Unknown	- -

CANADIAN CORPS CYCLISTS • 37

No.: 20-3-3   3RD DIVISIONAL CYCLIST COMPANY

The 3rd Divisional Cyclist Company was organized in February 1915 and received its authorization on January 22, 1916. It was disbanded on November 15, 1920.

DIVISIONAL CYCLISTS/3/CANADA OVERSEAS

AUTHORIZED JANUARY 22, 1916

Makers: Ellis
Fasteners: Lugs
Composition:
  Other Ranks: Browning copper; blackened copper
  Officers: Silver
Ref.: Babin 25-3, Cox 852

Badge No.	Insignia	Rank	Description	Extremely Fine
20-3-3-2	Cap	ORs	Browning copper	50.00
20-3-3-4		ORs	Blackened copper	50.00
20-3-3-21		Officers	Silver	150.00
20-3-3-41	Collars	ORs	Browning copper	20.00
20-3-3-43		ORs	Blackened copper	35.00
20-3-3-61		Officers	Silver	75.00
20-3-3-91	Shoulders	ORs	Title: "3/CYCLISTS"	

No.: 20-3-4   4TH DIVISIONAL CYCLIST COMPANY

The 4th Divisional Cyclist Company was organized on February 4, 1916, and disbanded on November 15, 1920.

4/CANADA/OVERSEAS/DIVISIONAL/CYCLIST/
VIRTUE ET LABORE

Makers: Bailey
Fasteners: Lugs, pin
Composition:
  Other Ranks: Pickled copper; browning copper
  Officers:
    A: Gilt on copper
    B: Silver
Ref.: Babin 25-6, Cox 853

Badge No.	Insignia	Rank	Description	Extremely Fine
20-3-4-2	Cap	ORs	Pickled copper; Bailey	75.00
20-3-4-4		ORs	Browning copper; Bailey	50.00
20-3-4-21		Officers	Gilt on copper; Bailey	175.00
20-3-4-23		Officers	Silver; Bailey	200.00
20-3-4-41	Collars	ORs	Pickled copper; Bailey	20.00
20-3-4-43		ORs	Browning copper; Bailey	15.00
20-3-4-61		Officers	Gilt on copper; Bailey	50.00
20-3-4-63		Officers	Silver; Bailey	50.00

No.: 20-3-5   5TH DIVISIONAL CYCLIST COMPANY

The 5th Divisional Cyclist Company was organized in June 1916, and was disbanded on November 15, 1920.

CANADIAN/DIVISIONAL/CYCLISTS

Makers: Gaunt
Fasteners: Lugs
Composition:
Other Ranks: Browning copper
Officers: Unknown
Ref.: Babin 25-2, Cox 850

Note: Collars are left and right.

Badge No.	Insignia	Rank	Description	Extremely Fine
20-3-5-2	Cap	ORs	Browning copper	250.00
20-3-5-21		Officers	Unknown	--
20-3-5-41	Collars	ORs	Browning copper	100.00
20-3-5-61		Officers	Unknown	--

No.: 20-5-1   CANADIAN CYCLIST DRAFT

CYCLISTS/CANADA/SILENT ET CELER

Makers: Birks, Unknown
Fasteners: Lugs
Composition:
  Other Ranks: Browning copper
       Officers: Unknown
Ref.: Babin 25-7, Cox 856

Badge No.	Insignia	Rank	Description	Extremely Fine
20-5-1-2	Cap	ORs	Unknown	- -
20-5-1-21		Officers	Browning copper; Birks	350.00
20-5-1-41	Collars	ORs	Unknown	- -
20-5-1-61		Officers	Unknown	- -

CANADIAN DEPOT BATTALIONS

The Canadian Depot Battalions were formed in August 1917 and established in central locations within various military districts across Canada. They handled the training of the final allotments of recruits and draftees to various battalions in England and fighting battalions in France. After the signing of the armistice, they were used as demobilization centres for returning Canadian corps. The battalions were disbanded on November 15, 1920.

Most depot battalions used the regiment badges of the military district in which they were posted, with the shoulder titles being the only identifying insignia.

They are listed below in the alphabetical order of the provinces in which they were located.

No.: 25-1-1

ALBERTA REGIMENT

1ST DEPOT BATTALION

Military District No. 13, headquarters in Calgary, Alberta

CANADA/DEPOT BATTN/ALBERTA REGIMENT

Makers: Unknown
Fasteners: Lugs, pin
Composition:
 Other Ranks: Browning brass
 Officers:
  A: Gilt on brass
  B: Silver
Ref.: Babin 38-6

Badge No.	Insignia	Rank	Description	Extremely Fine
25-1-1-2	Cap	ORs	Browning brass	250.00
25-1-1-21		Officers	Gilt on brass	500.00
25-1-1-23		Officers	Silver	500.00
25-1-1-41	Collars	ORs	Browning brass	100.00
25-1-1-61		Officers	Gilt on brass	150.00
25-1-1-63		Officers	Silver	150.00
25-1-1-91	Shoulders	ORs	Title: "IDBA/CANADA"	30.00

BRITISH COLUMBIA REGIMENT

No.: 25-2-1

Military District No. 11, headquarters in Victoria, British Columbia

1ST DEPOT BATTALION

DEPOT BATTN/1ST/BRITISH COLUMBIA

Makers: Allan
Fasteners: Lugs
Composition:
 Other Ranks: Browning copper or brass
 Officers: Unknown
Ref.: Babin 38-4, Cox 808

Badge No.	Insignia	Rank	Description	Extremely Fine
25-2-1-2	Cap	ORs	Browning copper	40.00
25-2-1-4		ORs	Browning brass	40.00
25-2-1-21		Officers	Unknown	- -
25-2-1-41	Collars	ORs	Browning copper	18.00
25-2-1-43		ORs	Browning brass	18.00
25-2-1-61		Officers	Unknown	- -
25-2-1-91	Shoulders	ORs	Title: "IDBBC/CANADA"	30.00

CANADIAN DEPOT BATTALIONS • 43

No.: 25-2-2

2ND DEPOT BATTALION

2ND DEPOT BATTN/REGI/BRITISH COLUMBIA

Makers: Allan, Unknown
Fasteners: Lugs
Composition:
  Other Ranks: Browning copper
  Officers: Unknown
Ref.: Babin 38-5, Cox 809

Badge No.	Insignia	Rank	Description	Extremely Fine
25-2-2-2	Cap	ORs	Browning copper; Allan	80.00
25-2-2-21		Officers	Unknown	- -
25-2-2-41	Collars	ORs	Browning copper; Allan	25.00
25-2-2-61		Officers	Unknown	- -
25-2-2-91	Shoulders	ORs	Title: "2DBBC/CANADA"	30.00
25-2-2-93		ORs	Title: "2ND DEPOT BN BC REGT./CANADA;" Allan	50.00

No.: 25-3

MANITOBA REGIMENT

1ST DEPOT BATTALION

Military District No. 10, headquarters in Winnipeg, Manitoba

MAN. DEPOT/1/BATTALION/CANADA

Makers: Unknown
Fasteners: Lugs
Composition:
  Other Ranks: Browning copper
      Officers: Unknown
Ref.: Babin 38-8, Cox 810

Badge No.	Insignia	Rank	Description	Extremely Fine
25-3-1-2	Cap	ORs	Browning copper	300.00
25-3-1-21		Officers	Unknown	--
25-3-1-41	Collars	ORs	Unknown	--
25-3-1-61		Officers	Unknown	--
25-3-1-91	Shoulders	ORs	Title: "IDBM/CANADA"	30.00

No.: 25-4

NEW BRUNSWICK REGIMENT
1ST DEPOT BATTALION

Military District No. 7, headquarters in Saint John, New Brunswick

SHOULDER TITLES ONLY

IDBNB/CANADA

Makers: Unknown
Fasteners: Lugs
Composition:
  Other Ranks: Brass
  Officers: Unknown
Ref.: Not previously listed

Badge No.	Insignia	Rank	Description	Extremely Fine
25-4-1-91	Shoulders	ORs	Title: "IDBNB/CANADA"	30.00

No.: 25-5-1

NOVA SCOTIA REGIMENT
Military District No. 6, headquarters in Halifax, Nova Scotia
1ST DEPOT BATTALION
1ST DEPOT Bn NOVA SCOTIA REGIMENT/CANADA

Makers: Scully
Fasteners: Lugs
Composition:
 Other Ranks: Brass; copper; white metal
 Officers: Gilt with silver overlay on design
Ref.: Babin 38-1, Cox 802

Badge No.	Insignia	Rank	Description	Extremely Fine
25-5-1-2	Cap	ORs	Brass, void	20.00
25-5-1-4		ORs	Copper, void	20.00
25-5-1-6		ORs	White metal, void	22.00
25-5-1-8		ORs	White metal, solid	22.00
25-5-1-21		Officers	Gilt, silver overlay on crown, maple leaf and Canada	135.00
25-5-1-41	Collars	ORs	Brass, void	10.00
25-5-1-43		ORs	Copper, void	10.00
25-5-1-45		ORs	White metal, void	12.00
25-5-1-47		ORs	White metal, solid	12.00
25-5-1-61		Officers	Gilt, Silver overlay on crown, maple leaf and Canada	40.00
25-5-1-91	Shoulders	ORs	Title: "IDBNS/CANADA"	30.00

No. - 25-5-2

REGIMENTAL DEPOT

NOVA SCOTIA REGIMENTAL DEPOT/ CANADA/CANADA/OVERSEAS

Makers: Unknown
Fasteners: Lugs
Composition:
  Other Ranks: Unknown
      Officers: Sterling silver
Ref.: Cox 803

Badge No.	Insignia	Rank	Description	Extremely Fine
25-5-2-2	Cap	ORs	Unknown	--
25-5-2-21		Officers	Sterling silver	300.00
25-5-2-41	Collars	ORs	Unknown	--
25-5-2-61		Officers	Unknown	--

No.: 25-6-1

1ST CENTRAL ONTARIO REGIMENT

Military District No. 2, headquarters in Toronto, Ontario

1ST DEPOT BATTALION

SHOULDER TITLES ONLY

IDBCO/CANADA

Makers: Unknown
Fasteners: Lugs
Composition:
  Other Ranks: Brass
  Officers: Unknown
Ref.: Not previously listed

Badge No.	Insignia	Rank	Description	Extremely Fine
25-6-1-91	Shoulders	ORs	Title: "IDBCO/CANADA"	25.00

No. - 25-6-2

2ND DEPOT BATTALION

SHOULDER TITLES ONLY

2DBCO/CANADA

Makers: Unknown
Fasteners: Lugs
Composition:
  Other Ranks: Brass
  Officers: Unknown
Ref.: Not previously listed

Badge No.	Insignia	Rank	Description	Extremely Fine
25-6-2-91	Shoulders	ORs	Title: "2DBCO/CANADA"	25.00

CANADIAN DEPOT BATTALIONS • 49

No.: 25-7-1

2ND CENTRAL ONTARIO REGIMENT
1ST DEPOT BATTALION
SHOULDER TITLES ONLY

IDB2CO/CANADA

Makers: General list
Fasteners: Lugs
Composition:
   Other Ranks: General list
   Officers: General list
Ref.: Not previously listed

Badge No.	Insignia	Rank	Description	Extremely Fine
25-7-1-91	Shoulders	ORs	Title: "IDB2CO/CANADA"	25.00

No. - 25-7-2

2ND DEPOT BATTALION
SHOULDER TITLES ONLY

2DB2CO/CANADA

Makers: General list
Fasteners: Lugs
Composition:
   Other Ranks: General list
   Officers: General list
Ref.: Not previously listed

Badge No.	Insignia	Rank	Description	Extremely Fine
25-7-2-91	Shoulders	ORs	Title: "2DB2CO/CANADA"	25.00

CANADIAN DEPOT BATTALIONS

No.: 25-8-1

EASTERN ONTARIO REGIMENT

Military District No. 3, headquarters in Kingston, Ontario

1ST DEPOT BATTALION

SHOULDER TITLES ONLY

IDBEO/CANADA

Makers: Unknown
Fasteners: Lugs
Composition:
  Other Ranks: Brass
    Officers: Unknown
Ref.: Not previously listed

Badge No.	Insignia	Rank	Description	Extremely Fine
25-8-1-91	Shoulders	ORs	Title: "IDBEO/CANADA"	25.00

No. - 25-8-2

2ND DEPOT BATTALION

SHOULDER TITLES ONLY

2DBEO/CANADA

Makers: Unknown
Fasteners: Lugs
Composition:
  Other Ranks: Brass
    Officers: Unknown
Ref.: Not previously listed

Badge No.	Insignia	Rank	Description	Extremely Fine
25-8-2-91	Shoulders	ORs	Title: "2DBE0/CANADA"	25.00

No.: 25-9-1

WESTERN ONTARIO REGIMENT

1ST DEPOT BATTALION

Military District No. 1, headquarters in London, Ontario

SHOULDER TITLES ONLY

IDBWO/CANADA

Makers: Unknown
Fasteners: Lugs
Composition:
 Other Ranks: Brass
 Officers: Unknown
Ref.: Not previously listed

Badge No.	Insignia	Rank	Description	Extremely Fine
25-9-1-91	Shoulders	ORs	Title: "IDBWO/CANADA"	25.00

1ST QUEBEC REGIMENT

No.: 25-10-1

Military District No. 4, headquarters in Montreal. Quebec

No. - 25-10-1A

1ST DEPOT BATTALION

FRENCH LEGENDS

*1ST REG DE QUEBEC/PREMIER BATTALION/
JE ME SOUVIENS/CANADA*

Makers: Caron, Rondeau
Fasteners: Lugs, pin
Composition:
  Other Ranks: Brass
    Officers: Gilt on brass
Ref.: Babin 38-2A

Badge No.	Insignia	Rank	Description	Extremely Fine
25-10-1A-2	Cap	ORs	Brass	35.00
25-10-1A-21		Officers	Gilt on brass	100.00
25-10-1A-23		Officers	Pickled brass, silver overlay on design	250.00
25-10-1A-41	Collars	ORs	Brass	50.00
25-10-1A-61		Officers	Gilt on brass	60.00
25-10-1A-63		Officers	Pickled brass, silver overlay on design	75.00
25-10-1A-91	Shoulders	ORs	Title: "IDBQ/CANADA"	30.00

No. - 25-10-1B

ENGLISH LEGENDS

1ST QUEBEC REGT/1ST DEPOT BATTALION/ JE ME SOUVIENS/CANADA

Photograph not available

Makers: Caron, Hemsley, Rondeau
Fasteners: Lugs, pin
Composition:
  Other Ranks: Brass
  Officers:
    A: Gilt on brass
    B: Pickled brass with silver overlay on design
Ref.: Babin 38-2

Note: Two makers of this cap badge exist:
  1. Hemsley — veined leaf
  2. Rondeau — pebbled surface on leaf

Badge No.	Insignia	Rank	Description	Extremely Fine
25-10-1B-2	Cap	ORs	Brass, large letters	40.00
25-10-1B-4		ORs	Brass, small letters	40.00
25-10-1B-21		Officers	Gilt on brass	100.00
25-10-1B-23		Officers	Pickled brass, silver overlay on design; Caron	250.00
25-10-1B-41	Collars	ORs	Brass	50.00
25-10-1B-61		Officers	Gilt on brass	60.00
25-10-1B-63		Officers	Pickled brass, silver overlay on design; Caron	100.00
25-10-1B-91	Shoulders	ORs	Title: "IDBQ/CANADA"	30.00

No.: 25-10-2

2ND DEPOT BATTALION

SHOULDER TITLES ONLY

Makers: Unknown
Fasteners: Lugs
Composition:
  Other Ranks: Brass
    Officers: Unknown
Ref.: Not previously listed

Badge No.	Insignia	Rank	Description	Extremely Fine
25-10-2-2	Shoulders	ORs	Title: "2DBQ/CANADA"	30.00

No.: 25-11-1

2ND QUEBEC REGIMENT

Military District No. 5, headquarters in Quebec City, Quebec

No. - 25-11-1A

1ST DEPOT BATTALION

FRENCH LEGENDS

*2EME REG DE QUEBEC/PREMIER BATTALION/
JE ME SOUVIENS/CANADA*

Makers: Hemsley, Rondeau
Fasteners: Lugs
Composition:
  Other Ranks: Pickled brass
  Officers: Pickled brass with silver overlay on design
Ref.: Babin 38-2A, Cox 805

Note: Two makers of this cap badge exist:
1. Hemsley — fine-veined leaf
2. Rondeau — pebbled surface on leaf

Badge No.	Insignia	Rank	Description	Extremely Fine
25-11-1A-2	Cap	ORs	Pickled brass; Hemsley	35.00
25-11-1A-4		ORs	Pickled brass; Rondeau	35.00
25-11-1A-21		Officers	Pickled brass, silver overlay on design; Hemsley	250.00
25-11-1A-41	Collars	ORs	Pickled brass; Hemsley	30.00
25-11-1A-43		ORs	Pickled brass; Rondeau	30.00
25-11-1A-61		Officers	Pickled brass, silver overlay on design; Hemsley	100.00
25-11-1A-91	Shoulders	ORs	Title: "IDB2Q/CANADA"	35.00

No. - 25-11-1B

ENGLISH LEGENDS

2ND QUEBEC REGT./1ST DEPOT BATTALION
JE ME SOUVIENS/CANADA

Makers: Hemsley, Rondeau
Fasteners: Lugs
Composition:
Other Ranks: Pickled brass
Officers: Pickled brass with silver overlay on design
Ref.: Babin 38-2, Cox 804

Note: Two makers of this cap badge exist:
  1. Hemlsey — fine-veined leaf
  2. Rondeau — pebbled surface on leaf

Badge No.	Insignia	Rank	Description	Extremely Fine
25-11-1B-2	Cap	ORs	Pickled brass; Hemsley	65.00
25-11-1B-4		ORs	Pickled brass; Rondeau	65.00
25-11-1B-21		Officers	Pickled brass, silver overlay on design; Hemsley	250.00
25-11-1B-41	Collars	ORs	Pickled brass; Rondeau	30.00
25-11-1B-61		Officers	Pickled brass, silver overlay on design; Hemsley	100.00

No.: 25-11-2 — 2ND DEPOT BATTALION

Military District No. 4, headquarters in Montreal, Quebec

No. - 25-11-2A

FRENCH LEGENDS

2EME REGT DE QUEBEC/DEUXIEME BATTALION/ JE ME SOUVIENS/CANADA

Makers: Rondeau
Fasteners: Lugs
Composition:
 Other Ranks: Pickled copper
 Officers: Pickled brass with silver overlay on design
Ref.: Babin 38-3A, 38-3, Cox 807

Badge No.	Insignia	Rank	Description	Extremely Fine
		Design With Buckle		
25-11-2A-2	Cap	ORs	Pickled copper; Rondeau	40.00
25-11-2A-21		Officers	Pickled brass, silver overlay on design; Rondeau	250.00
25-11-2A-41	Collars	ORs	Pickled copper; Rondeau	30.00
25-11-2A-61		Officers	Pickled brass, silver overlay on design; Rondeau	100.00
		Design Without Buckle		
25-12-2A-4	Cap	ORs	Pickled copper; Rondeau	40.00
25-12-2A-23		Officers	Pickled brass, silver overlay on design; Rondeau	250.00
25-12-2A-43	Collars	ORs	Pickled copper	30.00
25-12-2A-63		Officers	Pickled brass, silver overlay on design; Rondeau	100.00
25-12-2A-91	Shoulders	ORs	Title: "2DB2Q/CANADA;" Caron	30.00

CANADIAN DEPOT BATTALIONS • 57

No. - 25-11-2B   ENGLISH LEGENDS

*2ND REGT. OF QUEBEC/SECOND BATTALION/
JE ME SOUVIENS/CANADA*

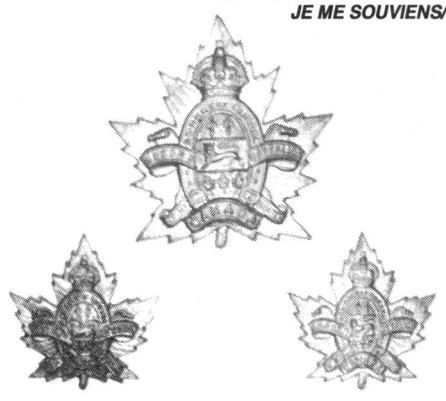

Makers: Hemsley, Rondeau
Fasteners: Lugs
Composition:
  Other Ranks: Pickled brass
  Officers: Pickled brass with silver overlay on design
Ref.: Babin 38-3, Cox 806

Note: Two makers of this cap badge exist:
  1. Hemsley — fine-veined leaf
  2. Rondeau — pebbled surface on leaf

Badge No.	Insignia	Rank	Description	Extremely Fine
25-11-2B-2	Cap	ORs	Pickled brass; Hemsley	40.00
25-11-2B-4		ORs	Pickled brass; Rondeau	40.00
25-11-2B-21		Officers	Pickled brass; silver overlay on design; Hemsley	250.00
25-11-2B-41	Collars	ORs	Pickled brass; Hemsley	55.00
25-11-2B-43		ORs	Pickled brass; Rondeau	55.00
25-11-2B-61		Officers	Pickled brass; silver overlay on design; Hemsley	100.00
25-11-2B-91	Shoulders	ORs	Title: "2DB2Q/CANADA;" Caron	30.00

No.: 25-11-3   **3RD DEPOT BATTALION**
              SHOULDER TITLE ONLY

              3DB2Q/CANADA

Makers: Unknown
Fasteners: Unknown
Composition:
  Other Ranks: Unknown
  Officers: Unknown
Ref.: Not previously listed

Badge No.	Insignia	Rank	Description	Extremely Fine
25-11-3-91	Shoulders	ORs	Title: "3DB2Q/CANADA"	30.00

No.: 25-12-1   **SASKATCHEWAN REGIMENT**

Military District No. 12, headquarters in Regina, Saskatchewan

1ST DEPOT BATTALION

SHOULDER TITLE ONLY

IDBS/CANADA

Makers: Unknown
Fasteners: Lugs
Composition:
 Other Ranks: Copper
 Officers: Unknown
Ref.: Not previously listed

Badge No.	Insignia	Rank	Description	Extremely Fine
25-12-1-91	Shoulders	ORs	Title: "IDBS/CANADA"	30.00

THE CANADIAN FORESTRY CORPS

In the early stages of the Great War, a farsighted Canadian lumberman, Alexander McDougall, approached the Imperial War Cabinet with a plan to organize a forestry corps in Canada, manned by skilled lumberman, for war service with the Allies. The concept and the offer of trained troops were declined by the War Cabinet. However, as the war progressed, it became increasingly evident that the Allied armies needed more and more timber and that a shortage would curtail Canada's overall war effort.

In February 1916, the Imperial War Cabinet sent a cable to the Governor General of Canada asking for a Canadian battalion to assist in the production of timber for war use, specifying that 1,500 trained men were urgently needed for this purpose. Within 25 days Canada had raised and outfitted the 224th Battalion (Canadian Forestry Corps) for this task, which was ready for work in the United Kingdom by April 12, 1916. Colonel McDougall, not wishing any delays in obtaining equipment, outfitted the new unit at his own expense from machinery firms in Canada and the United States at an initial cost of $250,000. By the beginning of November, the Canadian Forestry Corps had six units at work in the woods of the United Kingdom and France. The total strength of the corps was 23,979 men and they produced 70 percent of all timber used during the Great War.

Two infantry battalions of the Canadian Expeditionary Force were converted and absorbed into the Canadian Forestry Corps. They were the 224th Battalion (see page 63) and the 238th Battalion (see page 63). Four more Forestry Corps battalions were raised, as well as 101 forestry companies and depots from the various military districts in Canada, thereby giving the corps a national identity. Little or no records exist for the raising of these units, their strengths or their dates of disbandment.

No.: 30

No. - 30-1-1A

GENERAL SERVICE BADGE
WITHOUT "OVERSEAS"

CANADIAN FORESTRY CORPS (1917)

Makers: Gaunt
Fasteners: Lugs, tangs
Composition:
 Other Ranks: Browning copper
 Officers: Browning copper; superior construction
Ref.: Babin 34-3, Cox 916

Badge No.	Insignia	Rank	Description	Extremely Fine
30-1-1A-2	Cap	ORs	Browning copper; Gaunt	35.00
30-1-1A-21		Officers	Browning copper; Gaunt	35.00
30-1-1A-41	Collars	ORs	Browning copper; Gaunt	60.00
30-1-1A-61		Officers	Browning copper; Gaunt	60.00
30-1-1A-91	Shoulders	ORs	Unknown	--

THE CANADIAN FORESTRY CORPS

No. - 30-1-1B

WITH "OVERSEAS"

CANADIAN FORESTRY CORPS/OVERSEAS

Photograph not available

Makers: Tiptaft
Fasteners: Lugs
Composition:
 Other Ranks: Browning copper
 Officers: Browning copper
Ref.: Not previously listed

Badge No.	Insignia	Rank	Description	Extremely Fine
30-1-1B-2	Cap	ORs	Browning copper; Tiptaft	35.00
30-1-1B-21		Officers	Browning copper; Tiptaft	35.00
30-1-1B-41	Collars	ORs	Browning copper; Tiptaft	60.00
30-1-1B-61		Officers	Browning copper; Tiptaft	60.00

No. - 30-1-2

PIPERS' BADGE

CANADIAN FORESTRY CORPS

Makers: Unknown
Fasteners: Lugs
Composition:
 Other Ranks: White metal
 Officers:
Ref.: Not previously listed

Badge No.	Insignia	Rank	Description	Extremely Fine
30-1-2-2	Cap	Pipers	White metal	Rare

CANADIAN FORESTRY BATTALIONS

The Canadian Forestry Battalions were organized on July 17, 1917, and disbanded on November 15, 1920.

No.: 30-3-1

GENERAL SERVICE BADGES

TREE AND AXE DESIGN

CANADIAN FORESTRY BATTALION/OVERSEAS

Makers: Allan, Tiptaft, Unknown
Fasteners: Lugs, tangs
Composition:
Other Ranks: Pickled copper or brass; blackened brass
Officers: Unknown
Ref.: Babin 34-4, Cox see below

Large

Small

Note: Two makers of this cap badge exist:
 1. Tiptaft — large, 45mm. Cox 918
 2. Allan — small, 39mm, Cox 918

Badge No.	Insignia	Rank	Description	Extremely Fine
30-3-1-2	Cap	ORs	Pickled copper, large; Tiptaft	30.00
30-3-1-4		ORs	Pickled brass, small; Allan	30.00
30-3-1-6		ORs	Blackened brass, large; Tiptaft	35.00
30-3-1-21		Officers	Unknown	--
30-3-1-41	Collars	ORs	Pickled copper; Tiptaft	25.00
30-3-1-43		ORs	Pickled brass; Allan	75.00
30-3-1-45		ORs	Blackened brass; Tiptaft	75.00
30-3-1-61		Officers	Unknown	--

No. - 30-3-2   MODIFIED 238TH INFANTRY BATTALION

BLANK OVERLAY ON "238"

Makers: Hemsley
Fasteners: Lugs
Composition:
 Other Ranks: Pickled brass
    Officers: Unknown
Ref.: Not previously listed

Photograph not available

Badge No.	Insignia	Rank	Description	Extremely Fine
30-3-2-2	Cap	ORs	Pickled brass; Hemsley	125.00
30-3-2-21		Officers	Unknown	- -
30-3-2-41	Collars	ORs	Pickled brass; Hemsley	50.00
30-3-2-61		Officers	Unknown	- -

No. - 30-3-3   TREE AND SAW DESIGN

FORESTRY OVERSEAS BATTALION/CANADA

Makers: Hemsley
Fasteners: Lugs
Composition:
 Other Ranks: Pickled brass
    Officers: Pickled brass with white metal overlay on design
Ref.: Babin 34-5, Cox 921

Badge No.	Insignia	Rank	Description	Extremely Fine
30-3-3-2	Cap	ORs	Pickled brass	50.00
30-3-3-21		Officers	Pickled brass, Wm. overlay on design	150.00
30-3-3-41	Collars	ORs	Pickled brass	25.00
30-3-3-61		Officers	Pickled brass, Wm. overlay on design	50.00

224TH INFANTRY BATTALION

No.: 30-3-4

The 224th Battalion was raised in Eastern Ontario on July 15, 1916, under the authority of G.O. 69. Its mobilization headquarters was in Ottawa, Ontario. The battalion sailed for England on May 19, 1917, under the command of Lieutenant-Colonel A. McDougall, with a strength of 47 officers and 1,526 other ranks. In England the battalion was absorbed into the Canadian Forestry Corps. It was disbanded on September 15, 1920.

CANADIAN FORESTRY BATTALION/
224/OVERSEAS

Makers: Hemsley, Tiptaft, Unknown
Fasteners: Lugs
Composition:
Other Ranks: Pickled copper or brass
Officers:
  A: Silverplate
  B: Pickled copper with white metal overlay on design
Ref.: Babin, Meek, Stewart, Cox 760

Note: Two makers of this cap badge exist:
1. Hemsley *(illustrated)* — small central crown, thick numerals 224
2. Tiptaft — large central crown, thin numerals 224
The maker of the shoulder numeral 224 is not known.

Badge No.	Insignia	Rank	Description	Extremely Fine
30-3-4-2	Cap	ORs	Pickled copper; Hemsley	45.00
30-3-4-4		ORs	Pickled brass; Hemsley	45.00
30-3-4-6		ORs	Pickled brass; Tiptaft	45.00
30-3-4-21		Officers	Silverplate; Unknown	130.00
30-3-4-23		Officers	Pickled copper, Wm. overlay on design; Hemsley	100.00
30-3-4-41	Collars	ORs	Pickled copper; Hemsley	20.00
30-3-4-43		ORs	Pickled brass; Hemsley	20.00
30-3-4-45		ORs	Pickled brass; Tiptaft	20.00
30-3-4-61		Officers	Pickled copper, Wm. overlay on design; Hemsley	50.00
30-3-4-91	Shoulders	ORs	Numeral: "224"	--
30-3-4-93		ORs	Title: "224" over "CANADA;" Hemsley	20.00

No.: 30-3-5   **238TH INFANTRY BATTALION**

The 238th Infantry Battalion was raised in Ontario and Quebec on July 15, 1916, under the authority of G.O. 69. Its mobilization headquarters was at Valcartier, Quebec. The battalion sailed for England on September 11, 1916, under the command of Lieutenant-Colonel W.R. Smith, with a strength of 41 officers and 1,081 other ranks. In England the battalion was absorbed into the Canadian Forestry Corps. It was disbanded on September 15, 1920.

*CANADIAN FORESTRY BATTALION/
238/OVERSEAS*

AUTHORIZED JUNE 12, 1916

Makers: Hemsley, Tiptaft
Fasteners: Lugs
Composition:
Other Ranks: Pickled brass; blackened brass
Officers:
  A: Pickled brass with white metal overlay on design
  B: Pickled brass with white metal overlay on maple leaf and "238"

Ref.: Babin, Meek, Stewart, Cox 779

Note: Two makers of this cap badge exist:
  1. Hemsley *(illustrated)* — wide numerals 238, plain overseas ribbon
  2. Tiptaft — narrow numerals 238, framed overseas ribbon

Badge No.	Insignia	Rank	Description	Extremely Fine
30-3-5-2	Cap	ORs	Pickled brass; Hemsley	35.00
30-3-5-4		ORs	Blackened brass; Tiptaft	35.00
30-3-5-21		Officers	Pickled brass, Wm. overlay on design; Hemsley	100.00
30-3-5-23		Officers	Pickled brass, Wm. overlay on maple leaf and "238;" Hemsley	100.00
30-3-5-41	Collars	ORs	Pickled brass; Hemsley	25.00
30-3-5-43		ORs	Pickled brass; Tiptaft	25.00
30-3-5-61		Officers	Pickled brass, Wm. overlay on design; Hemsley	35.00
30-3-5-63		Officers	Pickled brass, Wm. overlay on maple leaf and "238;" Hemsley	35.00
30-3-5-91	Shoulders	ORs	Numeral "238"	--

CANADIAN FORESTRY COMPANIES

No.: 30-5-1

1ST FORESTRY COMPANY

"1" OVERLAID ON 224TH INFANTRY BATTALION BADGE

CANADIAN FORESTRY BATTALION/1/OVERSEAS

Makers: Unknown
Fasteners: Lugs
Composition:
   Other Ranks: Pickled brass
   Officers: Unknown
Ref.: Not previously listed

Note: Different styles of the overlay "1" exist.

Badge No.	Insignia	Rank	Description	Extremely Fine
30-5-1-2	Cap	ORs	Pickled brass, overlaid "1"	250.00
30-5-1-21		Officers	Unknown	- -
30-5-1-41	Collars	ORs	Pickled brass, overlaid "1"	100.00
30-5-1-61		Officers	Unknown	- -

No.: 30-5-2

2ND FORESTRY COMPANY

"2" OVERLAID ON 224TH INFANTRY BATTALION BADGE

CANADIAN FORESTRY BATTALION/2/OVERSEAS

Makers: Unknown
Fasteners: Lugs
Composition:
  Other Ranks: Pickled brass with "2" overlay
  Officers: Unknown
Ref.: Not previously listed

Badge No.	Insignia	Rank	Description	Extremely Fine
30-5-2-2	Cap	ORs	Pickled brass, overlaid "2"	250.00
30-5-2-21		Officers	Unknown	--
30-5-2-41	Collars	ORs	Pickled brass, overlaid "2"	100.00
30-5-2-61		Officers	Unknown	--

THE CANADIAN FORESTRY CORPS • 67

No.: 30-5-12   **12TH FORESTRY COMPANY**

The 12th Forestry Company was organized July 17, 1917, and disbanded November 15, 1920.

CANADIAN FORESTRY CORPS/12/OVERSEAS

Makers: Tiptaft, Unknown
Fasteners: Lugs
Composition:
 Other Ranks: Pickled copper;
  browning copper;
  blackened brass
 Officers: Unknown
Ref.: Babin 34-11, Cox 917

Badge No.	Insignia	Rank	Description	Extremely Fine
30-5-12-2	Cap	ORs	Pickled copper	55.00
30-5-12-4		ORs	Browning copper	50.00
30-5-12-6		ORs	Blackened brass	50.00
30-5-12-21		Officers	Unknown	- -
30-5-12-41	Collars	ORs	Pickled copper	40.00
30-5-12-43		ORs	Browning copper	40.00
30-5-12-45		ORs	Blackened brass	40.00
30-5-12-61		Officers	Unknown	- -

No.: 30-5-50

50TH FORESTRY COMPANY

FORESTRY OVERSEAS COMPANY/50/CANADA

Makers: Tiptaft, Unknown
Fasteners: Lugs
Composition:
 Other Ranks: Pickled brass; blackened brass
    Officers: Unknown
Ref.: Babin 34-12, Cox 924

Badge No.	Insignia	Rank	Description	Extremely Fine
30-5-50-2	Cap	ORs	Pickled brass	80.00
30-5-50-4		ORs	Blackened brass	75.00
30-5-50-21		Officers	Unknown	- -
30-5-50-41	Collars	ORs	Pickled brass	30.00
30-5-50-61		Officers	Unknown	- -

No.: 30-5-70

70TH FORESTRY COMPANY

CANADIAN FORESTRY CORPS/70TH CO/OVERSEAS

Makers: Tiptaft, Unknown
Fasteners: Lugs
Composition:
  Other Ranks: Blackened brass
  Officers: Unknown
Ref.: Babin 34-13, Cox 925

Badge No.	Insignia	Rank	Description	Extremely Fine
30-5-70-2	Cap	ORs	Blackened brass	200.00
30-5-70-21		Officers	Unknown	- -
30-5-70-41	Collars	ORs	Unknown	- -
30-5-70-61		Officers	Unknown	- -

No.: 30-5-80

BRITISH COLUMBIA FORESTRY COMPANY

Military District No. 11

CANADIAN FORESTRY BATTALION/OVERSEAS

Photograph not available

Makers: Allan, Unknown
Fasteners: Lugs
Composition:
  Other Ranks: Pickled copper
  Officers: Unknown
Ref.: Babin 34-8

Badge No.	Insignia	Rank	Description	Extremely Fine
30-5-80-2	Cap	ORs	Pickled copper	25.00
30-5-80-21		Officers	Unknown	- -
30-5-80-41	Collars	ORs	Pickled copper	20.00
30-5-80-61		Officers	Unknown	- -
30-5-80-91	Shoulders	ORs	Unknown	- -

No.: 30-5-82 **MANITOBA FORESTRY COMPANY**

Military District No. 10

The Manitoba Forestry Company was organized on July 17, 1917 and its personnel joined the Canadian Forestry Depot in England. This company did not proceed to frame as a unit. It was disbanded on November 15, 1920.

WINNIPEG FORESTRY CO/MD10/OVERSEAS/CANADA

Makers: Birks
Fasteners: Lugs
Composition:
 Other Ranks: Pickled brass
 Officers:
  A: Pickled brass; silver wash over design
  B: Pickled brass; gilt wash over design
Ref.: Babin 34-9, Cox 923

Badge No.	Insignia	Rank	Description	Extremely Fine
30-5-82-2	Cap	ORs	Pickled brass	300.00
30-5-82-21		Officers	Pickled brass, silver wash over design	1,200.00
30-5-82-23		Officers	Pickled brass, gilt wash over design	1,200.00
30-5-82-41	Collars	ORs	Pickled brass	75.00
30-5-82-61		Officers	Pickled brass, silver wash over design	200.00
30-58-2-63		Officers	Pickled brass, gilt wash over design	200.00

THE CANADIAN FORESTRY CORPS • 71

No.: 30-5-84 **NEW BRUNSWICK FORESTRY COMPANY**

Military District No. 8

"N.B." OVERLAID ON TIPTAFT GENERAL SERVICE CANADIAN FORESTRY BADGE, OVERSEAS VARIETY

CANADIAN FORESTRY BATTALION/NB/OVERSEAS

Makers: Tiptaft, Unknown
Fasteners: Lugs
Composition:
Other Ranks: Pickled copper with silver overlay on N.B.
Officers: Unknown
Ref.: Babin 34-7

Badge No.	Insignia	Rank	Description	Extremely Fine
30-5-84-2	Cap	ORs	Pickled copper, silver overlay on "N.B."	250.00
30-5-84-21		Officers	Unknown	- -
30-5-84-41	Collars	ORs	Pickled copper, silver overlay on "N.B."	Rare
30-5-84-61		Officers	Unknown	- -

No. - 30-5-86 **"N.B." OVERLAY ON 230TH BATTALION BADGE**

CANADIAN FORESTRY BATTALION/N.B./OVERSEAS

Makers: Hemsley
Fasteners: Lugs
Composition:
Other Ranks: Pickled copper
Officers: Gilt on copper with silver overlay on design
Ref.: Babin 34-7a, Cox 922

Badge No.	Insignia	Rank	Description	Extremely Fine
30-5-86-2	Cap	ORs	Pickled copper; Hemsley	500.00
30-5-86-21		Officers	Gilt on copper, silver overlay on design	200.00
30-5-86-41	Collars	ORs	Pickled copper; Hemsley	Rare
30-5-86-61		Officers	Gilt on copper, silver overlay on design	Rare

No.: 30-5-88   **NOVA SCOTIA FORESTRY COMPANY**

Military District No. 6

The Nova Scotia Forestry Company was organized on July 17, 1917, and was disbanded on November 15, 1920.

"N.S." OVERLAID ON 238TH BATTALION BADGE

CANADIAN FORESTRY BATTALION/N.S./OVERSEAS

Makers: Hemsley
Fasteners: Lugs
Composition:
 Other Ranks: Pickled brass
 Officers:
  A: Pickled brass; silver overlay on design
  B: Gilt on brass
Ref.: Babin 34-6, Cox 920

Badge No.	Insignia	Rank	Description	Extremely Fine
30-5-88-2	Cap	ORs	Pickled brass	150.00
30-5-88-21		Officers	Pickled brass, silver overlay on design	250.00
30-5-88-23		Officers	Gilt on brass	250.00
30-5-88-41	Collars	ORs	Pickled brass	35.00
30-5-88-61		Officers	Pickled brass, silver overlay on design	75.00
30-5-88-63		Officers	Gilt on brass	75.00

No.: 30-5-90

QUEBEC FORESTRY COMPANY

Military District No. 5

The Quebec Forestry Company was organized on July 17, 1917, and disbanded on November 15, 1920.

LES. FORESTIERS DE QUEBEC, C.E.F./JE ME SOUVIENS

Makers: Unknown
Fasteners: Lugs
Composition:
Other Ranks: Pickled copper; browning brass
Officers: Silver
Ref.: Not previously listed

Badge No.	Insignia	Rank	Description	Extremely Fine
30-5-90-2	Cap	ORs	Pickled copper; Unknown	300.00
30-5-90-4		ORs	Browning brass; Unknown	300.00
30-5-90-21		Officers	Silver; Unknown	1,100.00
30-5-90-41	Collars	ORs	Pickled copper; Unknown	Rare
30-5-90-43		ORs	Browning brass; Unknown	Rare
30-5-90-61		Officers	Silver; Unknown	Rare

CANADIAN GARRISON REGIMENTS AND BATTALIONS

No.: 35-1-1   **CANADIAN GARRISON REGIMENT**

CANADIAN GARRISON REGIMENT

Makers: Caron, Rondeau
Fasteners: Lugs
Composition:
Other Ranks: Copper; brass
Officers:
  A: Sterling silver
  B: Brass with sterling silver overlay on design
Ref.: Babin 37-1, Cox 826

Note: Three different makers of this cap badge exist:
1. Caron
2. Rondeau — flat badge
3. Unknown

Badge No.	Insignia	Rank	Description	Extremely Fine
35-1-1-2	Cap	ORs	Copper; Caron	20.00
35-1-1-4		ORs	Brass; Rondeau	25.00
35-1-1-21		Officers	Sterling silver; Caron	150.00
35-1-1-23		Officers	Brass, silver overlay on design; Rondeau	150.00
35-1-1-41	Collars	ORs	Copper; Caron	15.00
35-1-1-43		ORs	Brass; Rondeau	15.00
35-1-1-61		Officers	Sterling silver; Caron	50.00
35-1-1-63		Officers	Brass, silver overlay on design; Rondeau	50.00
35-1-1-91	Shoulders	ORs	Title: "C.G.R."	20.00

No.: 35-3-1   **BRITISH COLUMBIA GARRISON REGIMENT**

CANADIAN GARRISON REGT/BIIC

Makers: Allan
Fasteners: Lugs
Composition:
Other Ranks: Browning copper with browning copper overlay on "B11C"
Officers: Browning copper with white metal overlay of "B11C"
Ref.: Babin 37-2, Cox 827

Badge No.	Insignia	Rank	Description	Extremely Fine
35-3-1-2	Cap	ORs	Browning copper, browning copper overlay of "B11C"	60.00
35-3-1-21		Officers	Browning copper, Wm. overlay on "B11C"	125.00
35-3-1-41	Collars	ORs	Browning copper, browning copper overlay of "B11C"	30.00
35-3-1-61		Officers	Browning copper, Wm. overlay on "B11C"	50.00
35-3-1-91	Shoulders	ORs	Title: B.C. "CANADA"	20.00

No.: 35-5-4 **4TH GARRISON BATTALION**

CANADIAN GARRISON REGIMENT/4/ BATTALION/C.E.F.

Makers: Hemsley
Fasteners: Lugs
Composition:
 Other Ranks: Pickled brass
 Officers: Pickled brass with silver overlay on design
Ref.: Not previously listed

Badge No.	Insignia	Rank	Description	Extremely Fine
35-5-4-2	Cap	ORs	Pickled brass	150.00
35-5-4-21		Officers	Pickled brass, silver overlay on design	300.00
35-5-4-41	Collars	ORs	Unknown	- -
35-5-4-61		Officers	Unknown	- -

THE CANADIAN INTELLIGENCE CORPS

CORPS OF GUIDES

The Corps of Guides served from 1903 until 1929 as an element of the Non-Permanent Active Militia. A Canadian Corps Intelligence Section served in France as a unit of the Canadian Expeditionary Force during World War 1. The corps comprised of 499 personnel and 379 horses.

No.: 40-1-1 **GENERAL SERVICE BADGE**

GUIDES/CANADA/VIRTUE ET LABORE

Makers: Scully, Unknown
Fasteners: Lugs, slide
Composition:
  Other Ranks: Copper, brass
  Officers: Unknown
Ref.: Babin

Badge No.	Insignia	Rank	Description	Extremely Fine
40-1-1-2	Cap	ORs	Copper; Unknown	30.00
40-1-1-4		ORs	Brass; Unknown	30.00
40-1-1-21		Officers	Unknown	- -
40-1-1-41	Collars	ORs	Copper; Unknown	15.00
40-1-1-43		ORs	Brass; Unknown	15.00
40-1-1-61		Officers	Unknown	- -
40-1-1-91	Shoulders	ORs	Title: "Guides;" Scully	15.00
40-1-1-93		ORs	Title: "Scout"	15.00

THE CANADIAN MACHINE GUN CORPS

The machine gun was not a new weapon when the Great War began; its capabilities had been demonstrated effectively in the Russo-Japanese War. Unlike the British and French, the German Army realized the importance of the weapon and became the only European power to incorporate machine gun battalions into its military organization.

When war came in 1914, millionaire Raymond Brutinel, a French army reserve officer who was living in Montreal, in collaboration with a prominent lawyer, Clifford Sifton, hit upon the idea of mounting machine guns on armoured cars, thus providing the double threat of firepower and mobility. Sifton took their idea to the Minister of Militia, Colonel (later Sir) Sam Hughes, who enthusiastically endorsed the plans and authorized the organization of the 1st Canadian Automobile Machine Gun Brigade.

The brigade, which was privately financed, consisted of two batteries bearing the name Sifton, under the command of Brutinel, with a strength of ten officers and 124 other ranks. It had 24 Colt machine guns, eight armoured cars (built to Brutinel's specifications), eight trucks and four cars. By the end of the year three more batteries had been added: Eaton's, Borden's, and the Yukon.

No.: 45-1-1
GENERAL SERVICE BADGES
IMPERIAL ISSUE
CROWN AND CROSSED GUNS

Makers: Unknown
Fasteners: Lugs, Slide
Composition:
Other Ranks: Browning copper or brass
Officers:
  A: Silverplate on copper
  B: Gilt
Ref.: Babin 31-1, Cox 834

Note: Six different makers of these badges are identifiable by die variation. All makers are not identified.

Badge No.	Insignia	Rank	Description	Extremely Fine
45-1-1-2	Cap	ORs	Browning copper; Unknown	25.00
45-1-1-4		ORs	Browning brass; Unknown	25.00
45-1-1-21		Officers	Silverplate on copper; Unknown	50.00
45-1-1-23		Officers	Gilt; Unknown	50.00
45-1-1-41	Collars	ORs	Browning copper; Unknown	12.00
45-1-1-43		ORs	Browning brass; Unknown	12.00
45-1-1-61		Officers	Silverplate on copper; Unknown	25.00
45-1-1-63		Officers	Gilt; Unknown	25.00

No. - 45-1-3

CANADIAN ISSUE — STYLE A

CROWN AND CROSSED GUNS WITH CURVED CANADA RIBBON

CANADA

Makers: Gaunt, Unknown
Fasteners: Lugs, slide
Composition:
Other Ranks: Browning copper
Officers: Unknown
Ref.: Babin 31-3, Cox 836, 837

Note: Two varieties of this cap badge exist:
1. Gaunt — wide Canada ribbon with large "Canada"
   Cox lists this variety as badge for 3rd and 4th CMG Battalions
2. Unknown — narrow Canada ribbon with small "Canada"
   Cox Nos 836 and 837 are one and the same

Badge No.	Insignia	Rank	Description	Extremely Fine
45-1-3-2	Cap	ORs	Browning copper; Gaunt	30.00
45-1-3-4		ORs	Browning copper; Unknown	30.00
45-1-3-21		Officers	Unknown	- -
45-1-3-41	Collars	ORs	Browning copper; Gaunt	15.00
45-1-3-43		ORs	Browning copper; Unknown	15.00
45-1-3-61		Officers	Unknown	- -
45-1-3-91	Shoulders	ORs	Title: "MG/CANADA," browning copper (thick letters)	20.00
45-1-3-93		ORs	Title: "MG/CANADA," browning copper (thin letters)	20.00
45-1-3-95		ORs	Title: "C.M.G.C.," brass	20.00

THE CANADIAN MACHINE GUN CORPS

No. - 45-1-5

CANADIAN ISSUE — STYLE B

CROWN AND CROSSED GUNS WITH WAVEY CANADA RIBBON INSIDE GUNS

CANADA

Makers: Unknown
Fasteners: Lugs
Composition:
 Other Ranks: Browning copper
 Officers: Unknown
Ref.: Babin 31-4, Cox 840

Note: The illustrated badges are not a matched set.
There are three makers of ORs badges:
1. Unknown 1 — Skinny Vickers machine gun, four lugs
2. Unknown 2 — Fat Vickers machine gun, two lugs
3. Unknown 3 — Fat Vickers machine gun
The officers' badges have a solid back, bronze and are, possibly a Maxim, of good quality.

Badge No.	Insignia	Rank	Description	Extremely Fine
45-1-5-2	Cap	ORs	Browning copper; 4-lugs; Unknown 1	35.00
45-1-5-4		ORs	Copper; Unknown 2	35.00
45-1-5-6		ORs	Brass, 2-lugs; Unknown 3	35.00
45-1-5-21		Officers	Browning copper, 2-lugs	50.00
45-1-5-23		Officers	Browning copper, 4-lugs	50.00
45-1-5-41	Collars	ORs	Browning copper; Unknown 1	15.00
45-1-5-43		ORs	Copper; Unknown 2	15.00
45-1-5-45		ORs	Brass; Unknown 3	15.00
45-1-5-61		Officers	Browning copper	20.00
45-1-5-63		Officers	Browning copper	20.00

THE CANADIAN MACHINE GUN CORPS

No. - 45-1-7

CANADIAN ISSUE — STYLE C

CROWN, CROSSED GUNS, WITH WAVEY CANADA RIBBON BELOW GUNS

CANADA

Makers: Unknown
Fasteners: Lugs
Composition:
Other Ranks: Browning copper; brass
Officers: Unknown
Ref.: Babin 31-4, Cox 838

Note: These badges were constructed in one piece. The cap badges have outside ribbons and the collars have inside ribbons. The design characteristics of the cap badges must match those of the collars.

Badge No.	Insignia	Rank	Description	Extremely Fine
45-1-7-2	Cap	ORs	Browning copper	35.00
45-1-7-4		ORs	Brass	35.00
45-1-7-21		Officers	Unknown	--
45-1-7-41	Collars	ORs	Browning copper	20.00
45-1-7-43		ORs	Brass	20.00
45-1-7-61		Officers	Unknown	--

No. - 45-1-9 **CANADIAN ISSUE — STYLE D**

MAPLE LEAF DESIGN

CANADA

Makers: Tiptaft, Unknown
Fasteners: Lugs, tangs
Composition:
  Other Ranks: Brass
    Officers: Gilt on copper
Ref.: Babin 31-2, Cox 835

Note : Three varieties of this cap badge exist:
  1. Unknown 1 — large, heavy-veined leaf, with small ribbon
  2. Tiptaft — medium, lightly veined leaf, with large ribbon
  3. Unknown 2 — small, lightly veined leaf, with large ribbon
The officers' badge has a flat back.

Badge No.	Insignia	Rank	Description	Extremely Fine
45-1-9-2	Cap	ORs	Brass; Unknown-1	20.00
45-1-9-4		ORs	Brass, Tiptaft	20.00
45-1-9-6		ORs	Brass; Unknown-2	20.00
45-1-9-21		Officers	Gilt on copper; Unknown-1	25.00
45-1-9-41	Collars	ORs	Brass; Unknown-1	10.00
45-1-9-43		ORs	Brass; Tiptaft	10.00
45-1-9-45		ORs	Brass; Unknown-2	10.00
45-1-9-61		Officers	Gilt on copper; Unknown-2	15.00

CANADIAN MACHINE GUN COMPANIES

No.: 45-3-1   **1ST MACHINE GUN COMPANY**

The 1st Canadian Machine Gun Company was organized in November 1915 and absorbed into the 1st Machine Gun Battalion. No badges are known.

No.: 45-3-2   **2ND MACHINE GUN COMPANY**

In 1917 the 2nd Machine Gun Company was absorbed into the 1st Canadian Machine Gun Battalion.

2/CANADA

Photograph not available

Makers: Gaunt
Fasteners: Lugs
Composition:
  Other Ranks: Browning copper
  Officers: Unknown
Ref.: Not previously listed

Note: This badge was constructed in two pieces.

Badge No.	Insignia	Rank	Description	Extremely Fine
45-3-2-2	Cap	ORs	Browning copper; Gaunt	1,250.00
45-3-2-21		Officers	Unknown	- -
45-3-2-41	Collars	ORs	Unknown	- -
45-3-2-61		Officers	Unknown	- -
45-3-2-91	Shoulders	ORs	Unknown	- -

3RD MACHINE GUN COMPANY

No.: 45-3-3

3RD M.G.CO/1ST/CANADIAN/DIVISION

Makers: Tiptaft, Unknown
Fasteners: Lugs
Composition:
Other Ranks: White metal
Officers: Browning copper with white metal overlay on design
Ref.: Babin 30-3, Cox 839

Note: Two varieties of this cap badge exist:
1. Tiptaft — large size cap, 70 mm x 52 mm, white metal
2. Unknown — small size cap, 48 mm x 37 mm, white metal

Badge No.	Insignia	Rank	Description	Extremely Fine
45-3-3-2	Cap	ORs	White metal, large; Tiptaft	100.00
45-3-3-4		ORs	White metal, small; Unknown	100.00
45-3-3-21		Officers	Browning copper, Wm overlay on design, large; Tiptaft	850.00
45-3-3-41	Collars	ORs	White metal; Tiptaft	50.00
45-3-3-61		Officers	Browning copper, Wm overlay on design, small	100.00

4TH MACHINE GUN COMPANY

No.: 45-3-4

In 1917 the 4th Machine Gun Company was absorbed into 2nd Canadian Machine Gun Battalion.

4/MG/C/CANADA

Makers: Unknown
Fasteners: Lugs, slide
Composition:
  Other Ranks: Browning copper
  Officers: Unknown
Ref.: Babin 30-4, Cox 841

Badge No.	Insignia	Rank	Description	Extremely Fine
45-3-4-2	Cap	ORs	Browning copper; Unknown	350.00
45-3-4-21		Officers	Unknown	--
45-3-4-41	Collars	ORs	Browning copper; Unknown	150.00
45-3-4-61		Officers	Unknown	--

5TH MACHINE GUN COMPANY

No.: 45-3-5

The 5th Machine Gun Company was organized in November 1915. In March 1917 it was absorbed into the 2nd Canadian Machine Gun Battalion. No badges are known.

6TH MACHINE GUN COMPANY

No.: 45-3-6

The 6th Machine Gun Company was organized in November 1915. In March 1917 it was absorbed into the 2nd Canadian Machine Gun Battalion.

6/CANADA

Photograph not available

Makers: Gaunt
Fasteners: Lugs
Composition:
  Other Ranks: Browning copper
  Officers: Unknown
Ref.: Not previously listed

Badge No.	Insignia	Rank	Description	Extremely Fine
45-3-6-2	Cap	ORs	Browning copper; Gaunt	Rare
45-3-6-21		Officers	Unknown	--
45-3-6-41	Collars	ORs	Browning copper; Gaunt	Rare
45-3-6-61		Officers	Unknown	--
45-3-6-91	Shoulders	ORs	Unknown	--

No.: 45-3-9   **9TH MACHINE GUN COMPANY**

The 9th Machine Gun Company was organized in November 1915 and absorbed into the 3rd Canadian Machine Gun Battalion in March 1917.

9/CANADA

Makers: Unknown
Fasteners: Slide
Composition:
 Other Ranks: Browning copper or brass
 Officers: Unknown
Ref.: Babin 31-9, Cox 842

Note: Two varieties of this cap badge exist:
 1. Unknown 1 — one-piece construction with the 9 as an integral part
 2. Unknown 2 — two-piece construction, the 9 is added

Badge No.	Insignia	Rank	Description	Extremely Fine
45-3-9-2	Cap	ORs	Browning copper; Unknown 2	450.00
45-3-9-4		ORs	Browning brass; Unknown 1	450.00
45-3-9-21		Officers	Unknown	--
45-3-9-41	Collars	ORs	Browning brass	100.00
45-3-9-61		Officers	Unknown	--

No.: 45-5-1   **NEW BRUNSWICK MACHINE GUN DRAFT**

NEW BRUNSWICK MACHINE GUN
DRAFT C.E.F./CANADA

Makers: Unknown
Fasteners: Lugs
Composition:
  Other Ranks: Browning brass
  Officers: Sterling silver
Ref.: Babin 30-1

Badge No.	Insignia	Rank	Description	Extremely Fine
45-5-1-2	Cap	ORs	Browning brass; Unknown	1,000.00
45-5-1-21		Officers	Sterling silver; Unknown	1,500.00
45-5-1-41	Collars	ORs	Browning brass	Rare
45-5-1-61		Officers	Sterling silver	Rare

CANADIAN MOTOR MACHINE GUN BRIGADES

No.: 50-1-1   **1ST CANADIAN MOTOR MACHINE GUN BRIGADE**

The 1st Canadian Motor Machine Gun Brigade was organized on September 15, 1914, and disbanded on November 15, 1920.

1ST MOTOR MACHINE GUN/1914/CANADA/BRIGADE

Makers: Hemsley, Unknown
Fasteners: Lugs, pin
Composition:
  Other Ranks: Browning copper
  Officers:
    A: Silver plate on copper
    B: Gilt on copper
Ref.: Babin 29-1, Cox 829

Note: Two makers of this cap badge exist:
  1. Hemsley — the beaver has head up and a small tail
  2. Unknown — the beaver has head down and a large tail

Badge No.	Insignia	Rank	Description	Extremely Fine
50-1-1-2	Cap	ORs	Browning copper; Hemsley	250.00
50-1-1-4		ORs	Browning copper; Unknown	250.00
50-1-1-21		Officers	Silver plate on copper; Hemsley	300.00
50-1-1-23		Officers	Gilt on copper; Unknown	300.00
50-1-1-41	Collars	ORs	Browning copper; Hemsley	100.00
50-1-1-43		ORs	Browning copper; Unknown	100.00
50-1-1-61		Officers	Silver plate on copper; Hemsley	125.00
50-1-1-63		Officers	Gilt on copper; Unknown	125.00
50-1-1-91	Shoulders	ORs	Title: "1 MOTORS" over "C.M.G.C."	25.00

No.: 50-1-3 BORDEN'S MOTOR MACHINE GUN BATTERY

OTTAWA & NORTHERN ONTARIO

The Borden's Motor Machine Gun Battery was organized on July 1, 1915. From September 1915 to August 19, 1916, it was part of the 2nd Canadian Division. On August 19, 1916, it became associated with "C" Battery, of the 1st Canadian Motor Machine Gun Brigade.

B/AB/CANADA

Makers: Hemsley
Fasteners: Lugs, tangs
Composition:
Other Ranks: Pickled copper; browning copper
Officers: Pickled copper with silver overlay
Ref.: Babin 28-2, Cox 830

Badge No.	Insignia	Rank	Description	Extremely Fine
50-1-3-2	Cap	ORs	Pickled copper; Hemsley	150.00
50-1-3-4		ORs	Browning copper	225.00
50-1-3-21		Officers	Pickled copper, silver overlay on design	500.00
50-1-3-41	Collars	ORs	Pickled copper; Hemsley	50.00
50-1-3-43		ORs	Browning copper	50.00
50-1-3-61		Officers	Pickled copper, silver overlay on design	100.00

2ND CANADIAN MOTOR MACHINE GUN BRIGADE

No.: 50-3-1 **EATON'S MOTOR MACHINE GUN BATTERY**

TORONTO, ONTARIO

The Eaton Machine Gun Battery was mobilized on January 1, 1915, under the patronage of Sir John Craig Eaton and arrived in England on June 15. In January 1916 the name was changed to the Eaton Motor Machine Gun Battery. When the battery arrived in France on February 26, it served as part of the 3rd Canadian Division. From July 1916 to June 1918, it was transferred to the 1st Canadian Motor Machine Gun Brigade as D Battery, and the troops were allowed to wear their own badges. In June 1918 the battery was absorbed into the 2nd Canadian Motor Machine Gun Battery as B Battery.

No. - 50-3-1 **MAPLE LEAF DESIGN**

AUTHORIZED MARCH 23, 1915

E.M.G.B./CANADA

Small Beaver

Large Beaver

Makers: Unknown
Fasteners: Lugs
Composition:
 Other Ranks: Browning copper; blackened copper
 Officers: Unknown
Ref.: Babin 28-1, Cox 831

Note: Two different makers of this cap badge exist:
1. Unknown 1 — small beaver, 48 mm high
2. Unknown 2 — large, snarling beaver, 44 mm high

Badge No.	Insignia	Rank	Description	Extremely Fine
50-3-1-2	Cap	ORs	Browning copper; Unknown 1	200.00
50-3-1-4		ORs	Blackened copper; Unknown 2	240.00
50-3-1-21		Officers	Unknown	- -
50-3-1-41	Collars	ORs	Browning copper; Unknown 1	125.00
50-3-1-43		ORs	Blackened copper; Unknown 2	125.00
50-3-1-61		Officers	Unknown	- -
50-3-1-91	Shoulders	ORs	Title: "E.M.M.G.B./CANADA," browning copper	100.00
50-3-1-93		ORs	Title: "2 MOTORS" over "C.M.G.C."	25.00

CANADIAN MOTOR MACHINE GUN BRIGADES • 91

No. - 50-3-3

MAPLE LEAF CROSSED GUNS, DESIGN

CANADA

Makers: Gaunt
Fasteners: Lugs
Composition:
Other Ranks: Browning brass
Officers: Unknown
Ref.: Not previously listed

Badge No.	Insignis	Rank	Description	Extremely Fine
50-3-3-2	Cap	ORs	Browning brass; Gaunt	1,250.00
50-3-3-21		Officers	Unknown	--
50-3-3-41	Collars	ORs	Browning brass	20.00
50-3-3-61		Officers	Unknown	--
50-3-3-93		ORs	Title: "E.M.M.G.B./CANADA," blackened copper	100.00

No.: 50-3-5

BOYLE'S YUKON MOTOR MACHINE GUN BATTERY

YUKON, NORTH WEST TERRITORIES

Boyle's Yukon Motor Machine Gun Battery was raised on November 6, 1916, and arrived in France on March 25, 1918. It was absorbed into the new 2nd Canadian Motor Machine Gun Brigade as C Battery.

Y.T./CANADA

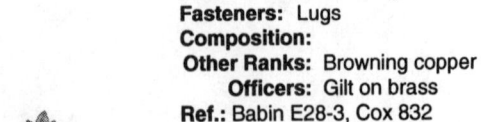

Makers: Gaunt, Jacoby
Fasteners: Lugs
Composition:
  Other Ranks: Browning copper
  Officers: Gilt on brass
Ref.: Babin E28-3, Cox 832

Badge No.	Insignia	Rank	Description	Extremely Fine
50-3-5-2	Cap	ORs	Browning copper; Gaunt	1,200.00
50-3-5-21		Officers	Gilt on brass; Jacoby	1,500.00
50-3-5-41	Collars	ORs	Browning brass; Gaunt	175.00
50-3-5-61		Officers	Gilt on brass; Jacoby	250.00

CANADIAN MOTOR MACHINE GUN BRIGADES • 93

No.: 50-5-1   **MISCELLANEOUS SHOULDER TITLES ONLY**

Makers: Various
Fasteners: Lugs
Composition:
  Other Ranks:
  Officers:
Ref.: Not previously listed

Badge No.	Insignia	Rank	Description	Extemely Fine
50-5-1-91	Shoulders	ORs	Title: "1 BDE/C.M.G.C."	25.00
50-5-3-91		ORs	Title: "3.BDE/C.M.G.C."	25.00
50-5-4-91		ORs	Title: "4.BDE/C.M.G.C."	25.00
50-5-5-91		ORs	Title: "5.BDE/C.M.G.C.	25.00
50-5-6-91		ORs	Title: "6.BDE/C.M.G.C."	25.00
50-5-7-91		ORs	Title: "7.BDE/C.M.G.C."	25.00
50-5-8-91		ORs	Title: "8.BDE/C.M.G.C."	25.00
50-5-9-91		ORs	Title: "9.BDE/C.M.G.C."	25.00
50-5-10-91		ORs	Title: "10.BDE/C.M.G.C."	25.00
50-5-11-91		ORs	Title: "11.BDE/C.M.G.C."	25.00
50-5-12-91		ORs	Title: "12.BDE/C.M.G.C."	25.00
50-5-13-91		ORs	Title: "13.BDE/C.M.G.C."	25.00

CANADIAN MILITARY, YMCA

The Canadian YMCA in France was a unit of the overseas military forces of Canada, with an authorized establishment of officers and other ranks.

No.: 55-1-1

YMCA MILITARY SERVICE

**CANADA/YMCA/OFFICIAL
MILITARY SERVICE DEPARTMENT**

Makers: Unknown
Fasteners: Lugs
Composition:
  Other Ranks: Browning copper
  Officers: Unknown
Ref.: Not previously listed

Badge No.	Insignia	Rank	Description	Extremely Fine
55-1-1-2	Cap	ORs	Browning copper	50.00
55-1-1-21		Officers	Unknown	- -
55-1-1-41	Collars	ORs	Unknown	- -
55-1-1-61		Officers	Unknown	- -
55-1-1-91	Shoulders	ORs	Title: "YMCA"	15.00

YOUNG MEN'S CHRISTIAN ASSOCIATION

No.: 55-1-3

CANADIAN DESIGN

CANADIAN/Y.M.C.A.

Makers: Unknown
Fasteners: Lugs, tangs
Composition:
Other Ranks: Browning copper
Officers: Gilt on copper, enamel
Ref.: Babin 39-12, Cox 930

Badge No.	Insignia	Rank	Description	Extremely Fine
55-1-3-2	Cap	ORs	Browning copper; Unknown	350.00
55-1-3-21		Officers	Gilt copper, enamel; Unknown	500.00
55-1-3-41	Collars	ORs	Browning copper; Unknown	35.00
55-1-3-61		Officers	Gilt copper, enamel; Unknown	75.00

No. - 55-1-5

PX DESIGN

SPIRIT BODY MIND/PX.

Makers: Unknown
Fasteners: Unknown
Composition:
Other Ranks: Browning copper with enamel overlay
Officers: Unknown
Ref.: Cox 931

Note: Other varieties exist.

Badge No.	Insignia	Rank	Description	Extremely Fine
55-1-5-2	Cap	ORs	Browning copper with enamel overlay	100.00
55-1-5-21		Officers	Unknown	- -
55-1-5-41	Collars	ORs	Browning copper with enamel overlay	25.00
55-1-5-61		Officers	Unknown	- -

THE CANADIAN PROVOST CORPS

THE CANADIAN MILITARY POLICE CORPS

The Canadian Military Police Corps was organized on October 15, 1917 and consisted of 13 detachments, two of which served with the Canadian Corps in the field. The duties of the Canadian Military Police Corps involved traffic control, investigations and managing detention camps, as well as maintaining discipline.

No.: 60-1-1   **GENERAL SERVICE BADGE**

No. - 60-1-1A   **"CMP" CYPHER DESIGN**

"CMP"/CANADIAN MILITARY POLICE

Makers: Birks, Unknown
Fasteners: Lugs
Composition:
  Other Ranks: Copper; brass
  Officers: Unknown
Ref.: Babin 35-2, Cox 943

Badge No.	Insignia	Rank	Description	Extremely Fine
60-1-1A-2	Cap	ORs	Copper; Birks	165.00
60-1-1A-4		ORs	Brass; Unknown	165.00
60-1-1A-21		Officers	Unknown	- -
60-1-1A-41	Collars	ORs	Unknown	- -
60-1-1A-43		ORs	Unknown	- -
60-1-1A-61		Officers	Unknown	- -
60-1-1A-91	Shoulders	ORs	Title: "CMPC;" Birks	10.00
60-1-1A-93		ORs	Title: "CMP," plain; Birks	10.00
60-1-1A-95		ORs	Title: "CMP"	10.00
60-1-1A-97		ORs	Title: "CMP," serifs	10.00
60-1-1A-99		ORs	Title: "CMP," (greatcoat)	20.00

No. - 60-1-1B   **"GVR" CYPHER DESIGN**

"GVR"/CANADIAN MILITARY POLICE

Makers: Tiptaft, Unknown
Fasteners: Lugs, slide
Composition:
 Other Ranks: Copper; brass
   Officers: Unknown
Ref.: Babin 35-1, Cox 944

Badge No.	Insignia	Rank	Description	Extremely Fine
60-1-1B-2	Cap	ORs	Copper; Tiptaft	150.00
60-1-1B-4		ORs	Brass; Tiptaft	150.00
60-1-1B-21		Officers	Unknown	- -
60-1-1B-41	Collars	ORs	Copper; Tiptaft	75.00
60-1-1B-43		ORs	Brass; Tiptaft	75.00
60-1-1B-61		Officers	Unknown	- -

CANADIAN MILITARY POLICE DETACHMENT

No.: 60-3-1   **1ST DETACHMENT**

LONDON, ONTARIO

The 1st Detachment was organized on October 15, 1917, and disbanded on December 1, 1920.

MILITARY POLICE/1/CANADA

Makers: Unknown
Fasteners: Lugs, tangs
Composition:
  Other Ranks: Brass
  Officers: Browning copper
Ref.: Babin 35-3, Cox 942

Badge No.	Insignia	Rank	Description	Extremely Fine
60-3-1-2	Cap	ORs	Brass	250.00
60-3-1-21		Officers	Browning copper	250.00
60-3-1-41	Collars	ORs	Brass	50.00
60-3-1-61		Officers	Browning copper	50.00
60-3-1-91	Shoulders	ORs	Title: "MILITARY POLICE/1/ CANADA OVER CANADA"	25.00

THE SPECIAL SERVICE COMPANIES

The Special Service Companies of the Canadian Expeditionary Force were employed mainly on guard and POW duties.

No.: 60-5-2   **2ND SPECIAL SERVICE COMPANY**

No. - 60-5-2A   **WITHOUT "C.E.F." DESIGN**

SPECIAL SERVICE/2/CANADA

Makers: Rosenthal, Unknown
Fasteners: Lugs
Composition:
  Other Ranks: Pickled copper
  Officers: Sterling silver
Ref.: Babin 36-2A, Cox 821

Badge No.	Insignia	Rank	Description	Extremely Fine
60-5-2A-2	Cap	ORs	Pickled copper; Rosenthal	185.00
60-5-2A-21		Officers	Sterling silver	300.00
60-5-2A-41	Collars	ORs	Unknown	--
60-5-2A-61		Officers	Unknown	--
60-5-2A-91	Shoulders	ORs	Unknown	--

100 • THE CANADIAN PROVOST CORPS

No. - 60-5-2B **WITH "C.E.F." DESIGN**

CEF/SPECIAL SERVICE/2/CANADA

Makers: Unknown
Fasteners: Lugs
Composition:
  Other Ranks: Browning copper
  Officers: Gilt on copper with enamel
Ref.: Babin 36-2, Cox 822

Note: Officers' gilt and enamelled badges were sometimes considered sweetheart pins.

Badge No.	Insignia	Rank	Description	Extremely Fine
60-5-2B-2	Cap	ORs	Browning copper	250.00
60-5-2B-21		Officers	Gilt on copper, enamel	300.00
60-5-2B-41	Collars	ORs	Unknown	--
60-5-2B-61		Officers	Unknown	--

No.: 60-5-3 **3RD SPECIAL SERVICE COMPANY**

C.E.F./SPECIAL SERVICE/3/CANADA

Makers: Unknown
Fasteners: Pin
Composition:
  Other Ranks: Pickled copper or brass
  Officers: Unknown
Ref.: Babin 36-3, Cox 823

Badge No.	Insignia	Rank	Description	Extremely Fine
60-5-3-2	Cap	ORs	Pickled copper	150.00
60-5-3-4		ORs	Pickled brass	150.00
60-5-3-21		Officers	Unknown	--
60-5-3-41	Collars	ORs	Pickled brass	75.00
60-5-3-61		Officers	Unknown	--

No.: 60-5-4   4TH SPECIAL SERVICE COMPANY

RSG/BRITISH COLUMBIA

Makers: Allan
Fasteners: Tangs, pins
Composition:
  Other Ranks: Browning copper
      Officers: Browning brass
Ref.: Babin 36-4, Cox 824

Badge No.	Insignia	Rank	Description	Extremely Fine
60-5-4-2	Cap	ORs	Browning copper	75.00
60-5-4-21		Officers	Browning brass, pin	85.00
60-5-4-41	Collars	ORs	Browning copper	25.00
60-5-4-61		Officers	Browning brass, pin	30.00
60-5-4-91	Shoulders	ORs	Unknown	- -

No.: 60-5-12   12TH SPECIAL SERVICE COMPANY

C.E.F./SPECIAL/12/SERVICE/CANADA

Makers: Unknown
Fasteners: Lugs
Composition:
  Other Ranks: Pickled brass;
      browning brass
      Officers: Unknown
Ref.: Babin 36-5, Cox 825

Badge No.	Insignia	Rank	Description	Extremely Fine
60-5-12-2	Cap	ORs	Pickled brass	775.00
60-5-12-4		ORs	Browning brass	600.00
60-5-12-21		Officers	Unknown	- -
60-5-12-41	Collars	ORs	Unknown	- -
60-5-12-61		Officers	Unknown	- -
60-5-12-91	Shoulders	ORs	Unknown	- -

THE CORPS OF CANADIAN RAILWAY TROOPS

In May 1918 the Overseas Railway Construction Corps and four independant companies — the 13th Light Railway Operating Company, the 58th Broad Gauge Operating Company, the 69th Wagon Erecting Company and the 85th Engine Crew Company — joined the 13 battalions serving out of the headquarters of the Canadian Railway Troops. The new body was called the Corps of Canadian Railway Troops.

CANADIAN OVERSEAS RAILWAY CONSTRUCTION CORPS

In the winter of 1915, the Imperial War Office requested that the Canadian Government send two railway construction companies to France. The Canadian Overseas Railway Construction Corps was organized on May 15, 1915, and comprised about five hundred men from the construction forces of the Canadian Pacific Railway Company. The unit sailed June 14, 1915. Two months later they landed in France.

In May 1916 the Imperial War Office asked Canada to furnish another railway construction unit of approximately one thousand strong. Recruits drawn from skilled railway workers across the country were organized into the 239th Overseas Railway Construction Battalion.

On June 15, 1917 the Canadian Overseas Railway Construction Corps was redesignated as the Corps of Canadian Railway Troops.

No.: 65 **GENERAL SERVICE BADGE**

No. - 65-1-1 *OVERSEAS RAILWAY CONSTRUCTION CORPS/CANADA*

Makers: Ellis, Tiptaft
Fasteners: Lugs
Composition:
Other Ranks: Browning copper
Officers:
    A: Browning copper with silver overlay on design
    B: Browning copper with browning copper overlay on design
Ref.: Babin 22-3, Stewart, Cox 870

Badge No.	Insignia	Rank	Description	Extremely Fine
65-1-1-2	Cap	ORs	Browning copper; Ellis	50.00
65-1-1-4		ORs	Browning copper; Tiptaft	50.00
65-1-1-21		Officers	Browning copper, silver overlay on design	100.00
65-1-1-23		Officers	Browning copper, Browning copper overlay on design	75.00
65-1-1-41	Collars	ORs	Browning copper; Ellis	25.00
65-1-1-43		ORs	Browning copper; Tiptaft	25.00
65-1-1-61		Officers	Browning copper, silver overlay on design	40.00
65-1-1-63		Officers	Browning copper, Browning copper overlay on design	30.00
65-1-1-91	Shoulders	ORs	Title: "Constr;" Ellis (1916)	20.00

CANADIAN CONTRUCTION BATTALIONS

No.: 65-3-1

1ST BATTALION

CANADA/OVERSEAS BATTALION/NO.1/CONSTRUCTION

AUTHORIZED JULY 11, 1916

Makers: Ellis, Tiptaft
Fasteners: Lugs
Composition:
Other Ranks: Pickled brass; blackened brass
Officers:
  A: Blackened brass with silver number
  B: Silver
Ref.: Babin 22-1, Cox 871

Note: Two varieties of this cap badge exist:
1. Ellis — Plain ribbons
2. Tiptaft — Framed ribbons

Badge No.	Insignia	Rank	Description	Extremely Fine
65-3-1-2	Cap	ORs	Pickled brass; Ellis	20.00
65-3-1-4		ORs	Blackened brass; Tiptaft	20.00
65-3-1-21		Officers	Blackened brass with silver number; Ellis	100.00
65-3-1-23		Officers	Silver; Ellis	100.00
65-3-1-41	Collars	ORs	Pickled brass; Ellis	16.00
65-3-1-43		ORs	Blackened brass; Tiptaft	16.00
65-3-1-61		Officers	Blackened brass with silver number; Ellis	30.00
65-3-1-63		Officers	Silver; Ellis	30.00

No.: 65-3-2

2ND BATTALION

CANADA OVERSEAS/NO.2/CONSTRUCTION

Makers: Unknown
Fasteners: Lugs, slide
Composition:
 Other Ranks: Pickled brass; browning brass
 Officers: Pickled brass with silver overlay on design
Ref.: Babin 22-2, Cox 872

Note: Two varieties of this cap badge exist:
  1. Unknown 1 — "No. 2" is plain and all ribbons have either no framing or very light framing
  2. Unknown 2 — "No. 2" is framed and all ribbons have heavy framing

Badge No.	Insignia	Rank	Description	Extremely Fine
65-3-2-2	Cap	ORs	Pickled brass; Unknown 1	30.00
65-3-2-4		ORs	Browning brass; Unknown 1	25.00
65-3-2-6		ORs	Browning brass; Unknown 2	25.00
65-3-2-21		Officers	Pickled brass, silver overlay on design	135.00
65-3-2-41	Collars	ORs	Pickled brass; Unknown 1	20.00
65-3-2-43		ORs	Browning brass; Unknown 1	15.00
65-3-2-45		ORs	Browning brass; Unknown 2	15.00
65-3-2-61		Officers	Pickled brass, silver overlay on design	100.00
65-3-2-91	Shoulders	ORs	Title: "NO.2/CONSTRUCTION/CANADA"	25.00

3RD BATTALION

239TH OVERSEAS BATTALION

No.: 65-3-3

The 239th Overseas Battalion was raised in Ontario and Quebec on July 15, 1916 under the authority of G.O. 69. Its mobilization headquarters was at Valcartier, Quebec. The battalion sailed overseas December 15, 1916, under the command of Major V. L. MacDonald, with a strength of 26 officers and 738 other ranks. In France it served as the 3rd Battalion, Canadian Railway Troops. It was disbanded on September 15, 1920.

No. - 65-3-3A

239TH BATTALION BADGE

*OVERSEAS RAILWAY CONSTRUCTION CORPS/
239/CANADA*

AUTHORIZED JULY 24, 1916

Makers: Birks
Fasteners: Lugs
Composition:
 Other Ranks: Pickled brass; browning copper
 Officers:
  A: Browning copper with silver overlay on "239"
  B: Pickled brass with white metal overlay on design
Ref.: Babin, Meek, Stewart, Cox 780

Note: Shoulder numerals "239" are not known.

Badge No.	Insignia	Rank	Description	Extremely Fine
65-3-3A-2	Cap	ORs	Pickled brass; Birks	85.00
65-3-3A-4		ORs	Browning copper; Birks	135.00
65-3-3A-21		Officers	Browning copper, silver overlay on "239;" Birks	350.00
65-3-3A-23		Officers	Pickled brass, Wm. overlay on design; Birks	400.00
65-3-3A-41	Collars	ORs	Pickled brass; Birks	75.00
65-3-3A-43		ORs	Browning copper; Birks	120.00
65-3-3A-61		Officers	Browning copper, silver overlay on "239;" Birks	120.00
65-3-3A-63		Officers	Pickled brass, Wm. overlay on design; Birks	120.00
65-3-3A-91	Shoulders	ORs	Numeral: "239"	- -
65-3-3A-93		ORs	Title: "BEAVER/239/CANADA"	50.00

No. - 65-3-3B   **MODIFIED 239TH BATTALION BADGE**

OVERSEAS RAILWAY CONSTRUCTION CORPS/3/CANADA

Makers: Birks, Unknown
Fasteners: Lugs
Composition:
 Other Ranks: Browning copper
    Officers: Unknown
Ref.: Cox 873

Note: This badge was modified from the 239th badge by cutting out the "2" and the "9" and leaving only the "3."

Badge No.	Insignia	Rank	Description	Extremely Fine
65-3-3B-2	Cap	ORs	Browning copper; Birks	500 .00
65-3-3B-21		Officers	Unknown	- -
65-3-3B-41	Collars	ORs	Unknown	- -
65-3-3B-61		Officers	Unknown	- -

CANADIAN RAILWAY TROOPS

In the latter part of 1916 it was agreed that Canada would furnish five battalions of construction workers to be known as the Canadian Railway Troops. In March 1917 it was decided to increase this number to ten battalions. By June all the battalions were at work in France.

No.: 65-5-1

1ST BATTALION

CANADA/FIRST OVERSEAS BATTALION/ RAILWAY CONSTRUCTION

Makers: Birks, Unknown
Fasteners: Lugs
Composition:
  Other Ranks: Browning brass
  Officers: Gilt on brass
Ref.: Babin 21-2, Cox 875

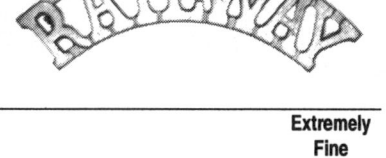

Badge No.	Insignia	Rank	Description	Extremely Fine
65-5-1-2	Cap	ORs	Browning brass	20.00
65-5-1-21		Officers	Gilt on brass	100.00
65-5-1-41	Collars	ORs	Browning brass	25.00
65-5-1-61		Officers	Gilt on brass	50.00
65-5-1-91	Shoulders	ORs	Title "Railway;" Birks (1915-1916)	20.00

No.: 65-5-2   **2ND BATTALION**

The 127th Infantry Battalion was raised in the County of York, Ontario, on December 22, 1915, under the authority of G.O. 151. Its mobilization headquarters was at Toronto. The battalion sailed overseas on August 24, 1916, under the command of Lieutenant-Colonel F. F. Clarke, with a strength of 32 officers and 972 other ranks. On November 8, 1916, it was redesignated as the 2nd Battalion, Canadian Railway Troops, and served in France in this capacity. It was disbanded on September 15, 1920.

No. - 65-5-2   *12TH REGT YORK RANGERS CELER ET AUDAY/*
                               CANADA 127 OVERSEAS

AUTHORIZED JANUARY 17, 1916

Makers: Birks, Caron, Ellis, Tiptaft
Fasteners: Lugs
Composition:
  Other Ranks: Picked copper; browning copper
  Officers:
    A: Pickled copper with silver overlay on "127"
    B: Browning copper with silver overlay on "127"
Ref.: Babin, Meek, Stewart, Cox 635

Note: Three makers of this cap badge exist:
1. Ellis *(illustrated)* — pointed-leaf design with plain ribbons and a lion with ears
2. Tiptaft — blunt-leaf design with framed ribbons and a lion without ears
3. Birks — blunt-leaf design with plain ribbons and a lion with ears

Badge No.	Insignia	Rank	Description	Extremely Fine
65-5-2-2	Cap	ORs	Pickled copper; Ellis	35.00
65-5-2-4		ORs	Browning copper; Ellis	25.00
65-5-2-6		ORs	Browning copper; Tiptaft	25.00
65-5-2-8		ORs	Browning copper; Birks	25.00
65-5-2-21		Officers	Pickled copper, silver overlay on "127;" Ellis	70.00
65-5-2-23		Officers	Browning copper, silver overlay on "127;" Tiptaft	70.00
65-5-2-25		Officers	Browning copper, silver overlay on "127;" Birks	240.00

THE CORPS OF CANADIAN RAILWAY TROOPS • 109

Badge No.	Insignia	Rank	Description	Extremely Fine
65-5-2A-41	Collars	ORs	Pickled copper; Ellis	16.00
65-5-2A-43		ORs	Browning copper; Ellis	16.00
65-5-2A-45		ORs	Browning copper; Tiptaft	16.00
65-5-2A-47		ORs	Browning copper; Birks	16.00
65-5-2A-61		Officers	Pickled copper, silver overlay on "127;" Ellis	20.00
65-5-2A-63		Officers	Browning copper, silver overlay on "127;" Tiptaft	20.00
65-5-2A-65		Officers	Browning copper, silver overlay on "127;" Birks	20.00
65-5-2A-91	Shoulders	ORs	Numeral: "127;" Caron	14.00
65-5-2A-93		ORs	Numeral: "127;" Birks	14.00

No. - 65-5-2B   *OVERSEAS BATTALION CANADA/127*

Makers: Caron for Eaton's
Fasteners: Lugs
Composition:
   Other Ranks: Pickled copper
   Officers: Pickled copper with white metal overlay on centre
Ref.: Not previously listed

Note: Collars are not known.

Badge No.	Insignia	Rank	Description	Extremely Fine
65-5-2B-2	Cap	ORs	Pickled copper; Caron	175.00
65-5-2B-21		Officers	Pickled copper, Wm. overlay on centre; Caron	275.00

No.: 65-5-3   **3RD BATTALION**

The 239th Battalion was converted and redesignated as the 3rd Battalion, Canadian Railway Troops, in February 1917.

CANADIAN RAILWAY TROOPS/3RD BN.

Makers: Unknown
Fasteners: Lugs
Composition:
Other Ranks: Browning copper with copper overlay on design
Officers: Browning copper with silver overlay on design
Ref.: Babin 21-3, Cox 877

Badge No.	Insignia	Rank	Description	Extremely Fine
65-5-3-2	Cap	ORs	Browning copper, copper overlay on design	50.00
65-5-3-21		Officers	Browning copper, silver overlay on design	150.00
65-5-3-41	Collars	ORs	Browning copper, copper overlay on design	25.00
65-5-3-61		Officers	Browning copper, silver overlay on design	75.00

4TH BATTALION

No.: 65-5-4

The 2nd Labour Battalion was redesignated as the 4th Battalion, Canadian Railway Troops, on June 15, 1917. The battalion was disbanded on November 1, 1920.

Makers: Gaunt
Fasteners: Lugs
Composition:
  Other Ranks: Browning brass; blackened brass
  Officers: Sterling silver
Ref.: Babin 21-4, Cox 878

Note: A mint badge must have the original red felt centre in place.

Badge No.	Insignia	Rank	Description	Extremely Fine
65-5-4-2	Cap	ORs	Browning brass; Gaunt	25.00
65-5-4-4		ORs	Blackened brass; Gaunt	20.00
65-5-4-21		Officers	Sterling silver	150.00
65-5-4-41	Collars	ORs	Browning brass; Gaunt	15.00
65-5-4-43		ORs	Blackened brass; Gaunt	15.00
65-5-4-61		Officers	Sterling silver	50.00

No.: 65-5-5   **5TH BATTALION**

The 3rd Labour Battalion was redesignated as the 5th Battalion, Canadian Railway Troops, on June 15, 1917. It was disbanded on November 1, 1920.

No. - 65-5-5A   **WREATH OF MAPLE LEAVES DESIGN**

CRT/5

Makers: C & S Co.
Fasteners: Lugs, tangs
Composition:
 Other Ranks: Browning brass
 Officers:
    A: Browning brass
    B: Gilt on brass
Ref.: Babin 21-5, Cox 879

Badge No.	Insignia	Rank	Description	Extremely Fine
65-5-5A-2	Cap	ORs	Browning brass, solid	100.00
65-5-5A-21		Officers	Browning brass, void	125.00
65-5-5A-23		Officers	Gilt on brass	125.00
65-5-5A-41	Collars	ORs	Browning brass, solid	30.00
65-5-5A-61		Officers	Browning brass, void	75.00
65-5-5A-63		Officers	Gilt on brass	40.00

No. - 65-5-5B   **MAPLE LEAF DESIGN, CRT 5 AND CANADA**

CRT/5/CANADA

Photograph not available

Makers: Unknown
Fasteners: Lugs
Composition:
  Other Ranks: Browning copper
  Officers: Unknown
Ref.: Not previously listed

Note: A collar of badge 100A was used as the overlay on a maple leaf with Canada embossed on it.

Badge No.	Insignia	Rank	Description	Extremely Fine
65-5-5B-2	Cap	ORs	Browning copper	150.00
65-5-5B-21		Officers	Unknown	- -
65-5-5B-41	Collars	ORs	Browning copper	50.00
65-5-5B-61		Officers	Unknown	- -

No.: 65-5-6   6TH BATTALION

The 6th Battalion was formed by the conversion and redesignation of the 228th Infantry Battalion at the Canadian Railway Troops depot in Purfleet, England. It was disbanded on November 1, 1920.

No. - 65-5-6A   **GRENADE DESIGN**

6/CANADIAN RAILWAY TROOPS

Makers: Gaunt, Unknown
Fasteners: Lugs
Composition:
Other Ranks: Browning brass
Officers:
    A. Browning copper
    B. Gilt on brass
Ref.: Babin 21-6, Cox 880

Badge No.	Insignia	Rank	Description	Extremely Fine
65-5-6A-2	Cap	ORs	Browning brass; Gaunt	85.00
65-5-6A-21		Officers	Browning copper; Unknown	125.00
65-5-6A-23		Officers	Gilt on brass; Gaunt	200.00
65-6-5A-41	Collars	ORs	Browning brass; Gaunt	40.00
65-6-5A-61		Officers	Browning copper; Unknown	40.00
65-6-5A-63		Officers	Gilt on brass; Gaunt	50.00

No. - 65-5-6B

MAPLE LEAF DESIGN

CANADIAN/6/RAILWAY/TROOPS

Makers: Gaunt
Fasteners: Lugs
Composition:
  Other Ranks: Browning brass
    Officers: Gilt on brass
Ref.: Babin 21-6. Cox 881

Badge No.	Insignia	Rank	Description	Extremely Fine
65-5-6B-2	Cap	ORs	Browning brass	100.00
65-5-6B-21		Officers	Gilt on brass	150.00
65-5-6B-41	Collars	ORs	Browning brass	50.00
65-5-6B-61		Officers	Gilt on brass	75.00

7TH BATTALION
257TH INFANTRY BATTALION

No.: 65-5-7

The 257th Infantry Battalion was raised in Eastern Ontario on July 15, 1916, with the authority of G.O. 69. Its battalion went overseas on February 16, 1917, under the command of Lieutenant-Colonel L. T. Martin, with a strength of 29 officers and 902 other ranks. It served in France as the 7th Battalion, Canadian Railway Troops and was disbanded on September 15, 1920.

No. - 65-5-7A

OVAL DESIGN

RAILWAY CONSTRUCTION/
OVER 257 SEAS/BATTALION/CANADA

AUTHORIZED JANUARY 18, 1917

Makers: Stanley & Aylward
Fasteners: Lugs
Composition:
  Other Ranks: Browning brass
  Officers: Unknown
Ref.: Not previously listed

Note: Shoulder numerals "257" are not known.

Badge No.	Insignia	Rank	Description	Extremely Fine
65-5-7A-2	Cap	ORs	Browning brass	175.00
65-5-7A-21		Officers	Unknown	- -
65-5-7A-41	Collars	ORs	Browning brass	50.00
65-5-7A-61		Officers	Unknown	- -
65-5-7A-91	Shoulders	ORs	Numeral: "257"	- -

No. - 65-5-7B **MAPLE LEAF ON CROWNED ANNULUS DESIGN**

OVERSEAS/CANADIAN RAILWAY TROOPS/
7/CANADA

Makers: Gaunt
Fasteners: Lugs
Composition:
Other Ranks: Blackened brass
Officers: Browning copper with silver overlay on design
Ref.: Babin 21-7, Cox 883

Badge No.	Insignia	Rank	Description	Extremely Fine
65-5-7B-2	Cap	ORs	Blackened brass; Gaunt	50.00
65-5-7B-21		Officers	Browning copper, silver overlay on design; Gaunt	125.00
65-5-7B-41	Collars	ORs	Blackened brass; Gaunt	40.00
65-5-7B-61		Officers	Browning copper, silver overlay on design; Gaunt	50.00

No.: 65-5-8   **8TH BATTALION**

The 8th Battalion was organized on June 15, 1917, at the Canadian Railway Troops depot in Purfleet, England. It comprised the 211th and 218th Infantry Battalions of the Canadian Expeditionary Force. The Battalion was disbanded on November 1, 1920.

Makers: Gaunt
Fasteners: Lugs
Composition:
 Other Ranks: Browning brass; blackened brass with red felt centre
 Officers: Sterling silver
Ref.: Babin 21-8, Cox 884

Badge No.	Insignia	Rank	Description	Extremely Fine
65-5-8-2	Cap	ORs	Browning brass; Gaunt	35.00
65-5-8-4		ORs	Blackened brass; Gaunt	35.00
65-5-8-21		Officers	Sterling silver	150.00
65-5-8-41	Collars	ORs	Browning brass; Gaunt	30.00
65-5-8-43		ORs	Blackened brass; Gaunt	30.00
65-5-8-61		Officers	Sterling silver	50.00

No.: 65-5-9

9TH BATTALION

The 9th Battalion was formed in 1917 by the conversion and redesignation of the 1st Pioneer Battalion into the Canadian Railway Troops.

OVERSEAS/1ST/CANADIAN PIONEERS

Makers: Tiptaft, Unknown
Fasteners: Lugs, slide
Composition:
Other Ranks: Pickled copper; browning brass
Officers: Unknown
Ref.: Babin 1-1, Cox 861

Note: Three makers of this cap badge exist:
1. Unknown 1
2. Unknown 2
3. Tiptaft

Badge No.	Insignia	Rank	Description	Extremely Fine
65-5-9-2	Cap	ORs	Pickled copper; Unknown	20.00
65-5-9-4		ORs	Browning brass; Unknown	30.00
65-5-9-6		ORs	Browning brass; Tiptaft	30.00
65-5-9-8		Officers	Unknown	- -
65-5-9-21	Collars	ORs	Pickled copper; Unknown	15.00
65-5-9-23		ORs	Browning copper; Unknown	15.00
65-5-9-25		ORs	Browning copper; Tiptaft	25.00
65-5-9-41		Officers	Unknown	- -

No.: 65-5-10   **10TH BATTALION**

256TH INFANTRY BATTALION

The 256th Battalion was raised in Central Ontario on July 15, 1916, under the authority of G.O. 69. Its mobilization headquarters was in Toronto. The battalion sailed overseas on March 28, 1917, under the command of Lieutenant-Colonel W.A. McConnell, with a strength of 18 officers and 531 other ranks. It served in France as the 10th Battalion, Canadian Railway Troops and was disbanded on September 15, 1920.

No. - 65-5-10A   **256TH BATTALION BADGE**

RAILWAY CONSTRUCTION OVERSEAS
BATTALION/256/CANADA

AUTHORIZED FEBRUARY 3, 1917

Makers: Roden, Unknown
Fasteners: Lugs
Composition:
  Other Ranks: Browning copper; blackened copper; antiqued copper
  Officers: Sterling silver
Ref.: Babin, Meek, Stewart, Cox 798

Badge No.	Insignia	Rank	Description	Extremely Fine
65-5-10A-2	Cap	ORs	Browning copper; Roden	75.00
65-5-10A-4		ORs	Blackened copper; Roden	75.00
65-5-10A-6		ORs	Antiqued copper; Roden	75.00
65-5-10A-21		Officers	Sterling silver; Roden	100.00
65-5-10A-41	Collars	ORs	Browning copper; Roden	60.00
65-5-10A-43		ORs	Blackened copper; Roden	22.00
65-5-10A-45		ORs	Antiqued copper; Roden	22.00
65-5-10A-61		Officers	Sterling silver; Roden	50.00
65-5-10A-91	Shoulders	ORs	Numeral: "256;" Unknown	50.00
65-5-10A-93		ORs	Title: "256RY" over "CANADA"	50.00

THE CORPS OF CANADIAN RAILWAY TROOPS • 121

No. - 65-5-10B

MODIFIED 256TH BATTALION BADGE

INTERIN DESIGN

10/CANADA

Makers: Gaunt
Fasteners: Lugs
Composition:
Other Ranks: Pickled brass; browning copper
Officers: Browning copper with silver overlay on number
Ref.: Not previously listed

Note: The cap and collars of badge no. 105A have "10" overlaid on "256."

Badge No.	Insignia	Rank	Description	Extremely Fine
65-5-10B-2	Cap	ORs	Pickled brass; Gaunt	65.00
65-5-10B-4		ORs	Browning copper; Gaunt	65.00
65-5-10B-21		Officers	Browning copper, silver overlay on number	150.00
65-5-10B-41	Collars	ORs	Pickled brass; Gaunt	40.00
65-5-10B-43		ORs	Browning copper; Gaunt	40.00
65-5-10B-61		Officers	Browning copper, silver overlay on number	75.00

No. - 65-5-10C **MODIFIED RAILWAY TUNNEL DESIGN**

10/C.R.T.

Makers: Unknown
Fasteners: Lugs
Composition:
   Other Ranks: Browning copper or brass
   Officers: Sterling silver
Ref.: Babin 21-10, Cox 886

Note: The dies were corrected by removing "256" and "Canada", and adding "10" and "C.R.T."

Badge No.	Insignia	Rank	Description	Extremely Fine
65-5-10C-2	Cap	ORs	Browning copper	25.00
65-5-10C-4		ORs	Browning brass	25.00
65-5-10C-21		Officers	Sterling silver	150.00
65-5-10C-41	Collars	ORs	Browning copper	20.00
65-5-10C-43		ORs	Browning brass	20.00
65-5-10C-61		Officers	Sterling silver	50.00

No. - 65-5-10D

MAPLE LEAF DESIGN

10/C.R.T.

Makers: Gaunt
Fasteners: Lugs
Composition:
Other Ranks: Pickled brass; browning copper
Officers: Browning copper with silver overlay on number
Ref.: Babin 21-10, Cox 887

Note: The collar badge is overlaid on a maple leaf to form the cap badge.

Badge No.	Insignia	Rank	Description	Extremely Fine
65-5-10D-2	Cap	ORs	Pickled brass; Gaunt	65.00
65-5-10D-4		ORs	Browning copper; Gaunt	65.00
65-5-10D-21		Officers	Browning copper, silver overlay on number	150.00
65-5-10D-41	Collars	ORs	Pickled brass; Gaunt	40.00
65-5-10D-43		ORs	Browning copper; Gaunt	40.00
65-5-10D-61		Officers	Browning copper, silver overlay on number	75.00

No.: 65-5-11 **11TH BATTALION**

The 11th Battalion was formed in the spring of 1918 by the conversion and redesignation of the 2nd Labour Battalion. It was disbanded on November 1, 1920.

Makers: Hicks, Unknown
Fasteners: Lugs
Composition:
Other Ranks: Browning brass with red enamel centre
Officers: Sterling silver with red enamel centre
Ref.: Babin 21-11, Cox 888

Badge No.	Insignia	Rank	Description	Extremely Fine
65-5-11-2	Cap	ORs	Browning brass, red enamel centre; Hicks	40.00
65-5-11-21		Officers	Sterling silver, red enamel centre	150.00
65-5-11-41	Collars	ORs	Browning brass, red enamel centre; Hicks	20.00
65-5-11-61		Officers	Sterling silver, red enamel centre	50.00

No.: 65-5-12   **12TH BATTALION**

The 12th Battalion was formed in the spring of 1918 by the conversion and redesignation of the 3rd Labour Battalion. It was disbanded on November 1, 1920.

CANADIAN RAILWAY TROOPS/12

Makers: Gaunt
Fasteners: Lugs
Composition:
Other Ranks: Browning copper; blackened copper or brass with red felt centre
Officers: Sterling silver with red enamel centre
Ref.: Babin 21-12, Cox 889

Badge No.	Insignia	Rank	Description	Extremely Fine
65-5-12-2	Cap	ORs	Browning copper, red felt centre	50.00
65-5-12-4		ORs	Blackened copper, red felt centre	50.00
65-5-12-6		ORs	Blackened brass, red felt centre	50.00
65-5-12-21		Officers	Sterling silver, red enamel centre	475.00
65-5-12-41	Collars	ORs	Browning copper, red felt centre	15.00
65-5-12-43		ORs	Blackened copper, red felt centre	15.00
65-5-12-45		ORs	Blackend brass, red felt centre	15.00
65-5-12-61		Officers	Sterling silver, red enamel centre	100.00

13TH BATTALION

No.: 65-5-13

The 13th Battalion was formed in the spring of 1918 from the personnel at the depot at Purfleet, England.

13/CANADIAN RAILWAY TROOPS

Makers: Service Supply
Fasteners: Lugs
Composition:
 Other Ranks: Blackened copper
 Officers: Sterling silver with enamelled crest
Ref.: Babin 21-13, Cox 890

Badge No.	Insignia	Rank	Description	Extremely Fine
65-5-13-2	Cap	ORs	Blackened copper	75.00
65-5-13-21		Officers	Sterling silver, enamelled crest	150.00
65-5-13-41	Collars	ORs	Title: "13/CRT"	100.00
65-5-13-61		Officers	Title: "13/CRT"	125.00

No.: 65-7-1 CANADIAN RAILWAY TROOPS DEPOT

The Canadian Railway Troops depot was organized on June 15, 1917, and disbanded on November 1, 1920.

CRTD

Makers: Unknown
Fasteners: Lugs
Composition:
Other Ranks: Browning copper
Officers: Browning copper with silver overlay "CRTD"
Ref.: Babin 21-14, Cox 891

Badge No.	Insignia	Rank	Description	Extremely Fine
65-7-1-2	Cap	ORs	Browning copper	450.00
65-7-1-21		Officers	Browning copper, silver overlay on "CRTD"	500.00
65-7-1-41	Collars	ORs	Browning copper	75.00
65-7-1-61		Officers	Browning copper, silver overlay on "CRTD"	100.00

No.: 65-9-1   1ST BRIDGING COMPANY

In August 1918 the 1st Bridging Company was formed for service in the Middle East. Six officers and 250 other ranks were selected from volunteers in France. They left for Palestine on September 20, 1918.

FIRST BRIDGING COMPANY
CANADIAN RAILWAY TROOPS

Makers: Unknown
Fasteners: Lugs
Composition:
 Other Ranks: Gilt on brass
       Officers: Unknown
Ref.: Babin 24-1

Badge No.	Insignia	Rank	Description	Extremely Fine
65-9-1-2	Cap	ORs	Gilt on brass	550.00
65-9-1-21		Officers	Unknown	- -
65-9-1-41	Collars	ORs	Gilt on brass	75.00
65-9-1-61		Officers	Unknown	- -

SKILLED RAILWAY EMPLOYEES

Badge No.: 65-11-1 **NO. 1 SECTION**

In May 1918 the No. 58 Broad Gauge Railway Operating Company was renamed the No. 1 Section of the Skilled Railway Employees.

N0. 65-11-1 *SKILLED RAILWAY EMPLOYEES/CANADA/ 1/SECT/OVERSEAS*

AUTHORIZED JANUARY 18, 1917

Makers: Gaunt
Fasteners: Lugs
Composition:
   Other Ranks: Pickled brass
   Officers: Browning copper with overlay on design
Ref.: Babin 23-1, Cox 892

Note: The officers' badge has a flat back and is thick and heavy.

Badge No.	Insignia	Rank	Description	Extremely Fine
65-11-1-2	Cap	ORs	Pickled brass	250.00
65-11-1-21		Officers	Browning copper, silver overlay on design	500.00
65-11-1-41	Collars	ORs	Pickled brass	90.00
65-11-1-61		Officers	Browning copper, silver overlay on design	100.00
65-11-1-91	Shoulders	ORs	Title: "SRE/CANADA," large	25.00
65-11-1-93		ORs	Title: "SRE/CANADA," small	25.00

Badge No.: 65-11-2 — NO. 2 SECTION

In May 1918 the No. 13 Canadian Light Railway Operating Company was renamed the No. 2 Section of the Skilled Railway Employees.

SKILLED RAILWAY EMPLOYEES/CANADA/2/OVERSEAS

Makers: Birks, Gaunt, Unknown
Fasteners: Lugs
Composition:
Other Ranks: Pickled brass
Officers:
  A: Browning copper with silver overlay on design
  B: Sterling silver
Ref.: Babin 23-2, Cox 893

Badge No.	Insignia	Rank	Description	Extremely Fine
65-11-2-2	Cap	ORs	Pickled brass; Unknown	250.00
65-11-2-21		Officers	Browning copper, silver overlay on design; Gaunt	500.00
65-11-2-23		Officers	Sterling silver; Birks	500.00
65-11-2-41	Collars	ORs	Pickled brass; Unknown	50.00
65-11-2-61		Officers	Browning copper, silver overlay on design; Gaunt	75.00
65-11-2-63		Officers	Sterling silver; Birks	75.00

Badge No.: 65-11-3 ## NO. 3 SECTION

In May 1918 the 69th Canadian Wagon Erecting Company was redesignated as the No. 3 Section of the Skilled Railway Employees.

SKILLED RAILWAY EMPLOYEES/3/CANADA

Makers: Gaunt
Fasteners: Lugs
Composition:
  Other Ranks: Blackened brass
    Officers: Browning copper
Ref.: Babin 23-3, Cox 894

Badge No.	Insignia	Rank	Description	Extremely Fine
65-11-3-2	Cap	ORs	Blackened brass	700.00
65-11-3-21		Officers	Browning copper	900.00
65-11-3-41	Collars	ORs	Blackened brass	50.00
65-11-3-61		Officers	Browning copper	75.00

Badge No.: 65-11-4 — NO. 4 SECTION

In May 1918 the 85th Canadian Engine Crew Company was redesignated as the No. 4 Section of the Skilled Railway Employees.

SKILLED RAILWAY EMPLOYEES/4/SECT/CANADA

Photograph not available

Makers: Gaunt
Fasteners: Lugs
Composition:
  Other Ranks: Blackened brass
  Officers: Browning copper with flat back
Ref.: Babin 23-4, Cox 895

Badge No.	Insignia	Rank	Description	Extremely Fine
65-11-4-2	Cap	ORs	Blackened brass	Rare
65-11-4-21		Officers	Browning copper, flat back	Rare
65-11-4-41	Collars	ORs	Blackened brass	Rare
65-11-4-61		Officers	Browning copper, flat back	Rare

THE CORPS OF ROYAL CANADIAN ENGINEERS

CANADIAN ENGINEERS

The Canadian Engineers was responsible for all defensive measures, including wiring, trenches, gun enplacements, offensive and defensive mining subways, roads, bridges, railways, medical accommodations, water supply and purification and numerous other vital tasks. All accommodation and storage huts were built by the engineers and they were also charged with maintaining sanitation standards.

Captain Coulson Norman Mitchell of the Corps of Royal Canadian Engineers was awarded the Victoria Cross for his bravery at Canla de l'Escaut on October 8 and 9, 1918.

No.: 70-1-1

GENERAL SERVICE BADGE

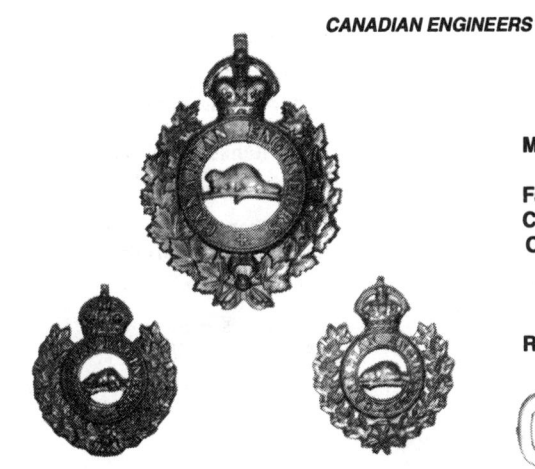

CANADIAN ENGINEERS

Makers: Caron, Gaunt, Roden, Tiptaft, Unknown
Fasteners: Lugs
Composition:
Other Ranks: Pickled brass; browning copper or brass
Officers: Gilt on brass
Ref.: Cox 858, 857

Note: There are more than six makers of the Canadian Engineers badge.

Badge No.	Insignia	Rank	Description	Extremely Fine
70-1-1-2	Cap	ORs	Pickled brass	15.00
70-1-1-4		ORs	Browning copper	15.00
70-1-1-6		ORs	Browning brass	15.00
70-1-1-21		Officers	Gilt on brass	50.00
70-1-1-41	Collars	ORs	Pickled brass	10.00
70-1-1-43		ORs	Browning copper	10.00
70-1-1-45		ORs	Browning brass	10.00
70-1-1-61		Officers	Gilt on brass	25.00
70-1-1-91	Shoulders	ORs	Title: "C.E."	10.00

CANADIAN PIONEER BATTALIONS

Canada's eight Pioneer Battalions performed the same kind of duties as the engineers. Often working closely with the engineers, the Pioneers helped maintain open lines of communication. All the Pioneer Battalions, except the 1st Pioneer Battalion, were absorbed into the Canadian Engineers upon reorganization of that corps in 1917.

No.: 70-3-1   **1ST PIONEER BATTALION**

The 1st Pioneer Battalion was organized on December 22, 1915. When the other Pioneer Battalions were absorbed into the Canadian Engineers, this battalion became part of the Canadian Railway Troops. It was disbanded in March 1917.

OVERSEAS/1ST/CANADIAN PIONEERS

Makers: Tiptaft, Unknown
Fasteners: Lugs, slide
Composition:
Other Ranks: Pickled copper; browning copper or brass
Officers: Unknown
Ref.: Babin 1-1, Cox 861

Note: Three makers of this cap badge exist:
1. Unknown 1
2. Unknown 2
3. Tiptaft

Badge No.	Insignia	Rank	Description	Extremely Fine
70-3-1-2	Cap	ORs	Pickled copper; Unknown	20.00
70-3-1-4		ORs	Browning brass; Unknown	20.00
70-3-1-6		ORs	Browning brass; Tiptaft	20.00
70-3-1-21		Officers	Unknown	- -
70-3-1-41	Collars	ORs	Pickled copper; Unknown	15.00
70-3-1-43		ORs	Browning copper; Unknown	15.00
70-3-1-45		ORs	Browning copper; Tiptaft	25.00
70-3-1-61		Officers	Unknown	- -
70-3-1-91	Shoulders	ORs	Title: "1ST CANADIAN PIONEERS"	25.00
70-3-1-93		ORs	Title: "PIONEERS"	20.00
70-3-1-95	Sleeves	ORs	Rifle and a pick	25.00

2ND PIONEER BATTALION

No.: 70-3-2

The 2nd Pioneer Battalion was organized on December 22, 1915, and disbanded in March 1918.

OVERSEAS/2ND CANADIAN PIONEER BATTALION/
VIAM PARAMUS

Makers: Birks, Tiptaft
Fasteners: Lugs
Composition:
Other Ranks: Pickled copper; browning copper
Officers: Unknown
Ref.: Babin 1-2, Cox 862

Note: Two makers of this cap badge exist:
  1. Birks — plain ribbons
  2. Tiptaft — framed ribbons

Badge No.	Insignia	Rank	Description	Extremely Fine
70-3-2-2	Cap	ORs	Pickled copper, Birks	20.00
70-3-2-4		ORs	Browning copper; Birks	20.00
70-3-2-6		ORs	Browning copper; Tiptaft	20.00
70-3-2-21		Officers	Unknown	--
70-3-2-41	Collars	ORs	Pickled copper; Birks	10.00
70-3-2-43		ORs	Browning copper; Birks	10.00
70-3-2-45		ORs	Browning copper; Tiptaft	10.00
70-3-2-61		Officers	Unknown	--

No.: 70-3-3   **3RD PIONEER BATTALION**

The 3rd Pioneer Battalion was organized on July 15, 1916, and disbanded in March 1918.

SPLENDOR SINE OCCASU/48TH C.E.F./
CANADIAN 3 PIONEERS

Makers: Allan, Tiptaft
Fasteners: Lugs, tangs
Composition:
  Other Ranks: Browning brass; blackened brass
    Officers: Unknown
Ref.: Babin 1-3, Cox 863

Badge No.	Insignia	Rank	Description	Extremely Fine
70-3-3-2	Cap	ORs	Browning brass	20.00
70-3-3-4		ORs	Blackened brass	20.00
70-3-3-21		Officers	Unknown	- -
70-3-3-41	Collars	ORs	Browning brass	10.00
70-3-3-43		ORs	Blackened brass	10.00
70-3-3-61		Officers	Unknown	- -
70-3-3-91	Shoulders	ORs	Title: "B.C. PIONEERS CANADA"	25.00

No.: 70-3-4

4TH PIONEER BATTALION

the 4th Pioneer Battalion was organized on July 15, 1916, and disbanded in March 1918.

CANADA/4/OVERSEAS PIONEER BATTALION

Makers: Birks, Tiptaft
Fasteners: Lugs, tangs, pin
Composition:
Other Ranks: Pickled copper or brass; browning copper or brass
Officers: Pickled copper with silver overlay on design
Ref.: Babin 1-4, Cox 865 solid, 864 void

Note: Two makers of this cap badge exist:
1. Birks — plain ribbons, void
2. Tiptaft — framed ribbons, solid

Badge No.	Insignia	Rank	Description	Extremely Fine
70-3-4-2	Cap	ORs	Pickled copper, void; Birks	25.00
70-3-4-4		ORs	Pickled brass, void; Birks	25.00
70-3-4-6		ORs	Browning copper, void; Birks	25.00
70-3-4-8		ORs	Browning copper, solid; Tiptaft	25.00
70-3-4-21		Officers	Pickled copper, silver overlay on design, void; Birks	125.00
70-3-4-41	Collars	ORs	Pickled copper, void; Birks	12.00
70-3-4-43		ORs	Browning copper, void; Birks	12.00
70-3-4-45		ORs	Browning brass, solid; Tiptaft	30.00
70-3-4-61		Officers	Pickled copper, silver overlay on design, void; Birks	50.00

No.: 70-3-5   **5TH PIONEER BATTALION**

The 5th Pioneer Battalion was organized on July 15, 1916, and disbanded in March 1918.

OVERSEAS PIONEER BATTALION/5/CANADA/
SEDMILES SED PRO PATRIA

Makers: Hemsley, Tiptaft
Fasteners: Lugs
Composition:
Other Ranks: Pickled copper; browning copper
Officers: Pickled copper with silver overlay on design
Ref.: Babin 1-5, Cox 866

Note: Two makers of this cap badge exist:
1. Hemsley — pointed leaf and plain ribbons
2. Tiptaft — blunt leaf and framed ribbons

Badge No.	Insignia	Rank	Description	Extremely Fine
70-3-5-2	Cap	ORs	Pickled copper; Hemsley	20.00
70-3-5-4		ORs	Browning copper; Tiptaft	20.00
70-3-5-21		Officers	Pickled copper, Silver overlay on design; Hemsley	75.00
70-3-5-41	Collars	ORs	Pickled copper; Hemsley	10.00
70-3-5-43		ORs	Browning copper; Tiptaft	10.00
70-3-5-61		Officers	Pickled copper, Silver overlay on design; Hemsley	40.00

107TH PIONEER BATTALION

The Battalion was raised and mobilized in Winnipeg, Manitoba under the authority of G.O. 151 December 22, 1915. The Battalion sailed on September 19, 1916 under the command of Lieutenant-Colonel G. Campbell with a strength of 32 officers and 965 other ranks. In England the Battalion was redesignated the 107th Pioneer Battalion and served in France in that capacity. It was disbanded on September 15, 1920.

No.: 70-3-107 **WINNIPEG BATTALION**

OVERSEAS/107/BATTALION/WINNIPEG

Makers: Dingwall, Tiptaft
Fasteners: Lugs
Composition:
Other Ranks: Pickled brass; browning copper; blackened brass
Officers: Sterling silver
Ref.: Babin, Meek, Stewart, Cox 609

Note: Two makers of this cap badge exist:
   1. Dingwall (*illustrated*) — thick type for numbers, large type for letters
   2. Tiptaft — narrow type for numbers, small type for letter

Badge No.	Insignia	Rank	Description	Extremely Fine
70-3-107-2	Cap	ORs	Pickled brass; Dingwall	25.00
70-3-107-4		ORs	Browning copper; Dingwall	25.00
70-3-107-6		ORs	Blackened brass; Tiptaft	25.00
70-3-107-21		Officers	Sterling silver	125.00
70-3-107-41	Collars	ORs	Pickled brass; Dingwall	25.00
70-3-107-43		ORs	Browning copper	25.00
70-3-107-43		ORs	Blackened brass	25.00
70-3-107-61		Officers	Sterling silver	125.00
70-3-107-91	Shoulders	ORs	Numeral: "107"; Caron	14.00
70-3-107-93		ORs	Title: "INF. 107 BATT/CANADA"; Dingwall	25.00

123RD PIONEER BATTALION

No.: 70-3-123

The 123rd Infantry battalion was raised in Toronto, Ontario, on December 22, 1915, under the authority of G.O. 151. It was mobilized in Toronto and sailed overseas on August 9, 1916, under the command of Lieutenant-Colonel W.B. Kingsmill, with a strength of 12 officers and 369 other ranks. In England the battalion was redesignated as the 123rd Pioneer Battalion. It was disbanded on September 15, 1920.

No. - 70-3-123A   *HONI SOIT QUI MAL Y PENSE/*
                         READY AYE READY/
                   CANADA OVERSEAS/123/ROYAL GRENADIERS

Makers: Birks, Caron, Ellis, Tiptaft, Unknown
Fasteners: Lugs
Composition:
Other Ranks: Browning copper; blackened copper or brass
Officers:
   A: Gilt on copper
   B: Gilt on brass
   C: Sterling silver
Ref.: Babin, Meek, Stewart, Cox

Note: Two makers of this cap badge exist:
   1. Ellis *(illustrated)* — the "3" in "123" has blunt serifs, plain ribbons
   2. Tiptaft — the "3" in "123" has pointed serifs, framed ribbons

Badge No.	Insignia	Rank	Description	Extremely Fine
70-3-123A-2	Cap	ORs	Browning copper; Ellis	18.00
70-3-123A-4		ORs	Blackened copper; Tiptaft	24.00
70-3-123A-6		ORs	Blackened brass; Ellis	24.00
70-3-123A-21		Officers	Gilt on copper; Unknown	85.00
70-3-123A-23		Officers	Sterling silver; Ellis	100.00
70-3-123A-41	Collars	ORs	Brass, horizontal; Ellis	30.00
70-3-123A-43		ORs	Brass, horizontal; Tiptaft	30.00
70-3-123A-45		NCO	Gilt on brass, horizontal; Ellis	35.00
70-3-123A-47		NCO	Gilt on brass, horizontal; Tiptaft	35.00
70-3-123A-61		Officers	Gilt on brass, perpendicular; Unknown	35.00
70-3-123A-63		Officers	Gilt on brass, perpendicular; Tiptaft	35.00
70-3-123A-91	Shoulders	ORs	Numeral: "123"; Caron	14.00
70-3-123A-93		ORs	Numeral: "123"; Birks	14.00
70-3-123A-95		ORs	Numeral: "123"; Tiptaft	14.00

No. - 70-3-123B   **OVERSEAS BATTALION CANADA/123**

Makers: Caron for Eaton's
Fasteners: Lugs, pin
Composition:
Other Ranks: Pickled copper
Officers: Pickled copper with white metal overlay on centre
Ref.: Not previously listed

Note: Collars not issued.

Badge No.	Insignia	Rank	Description	Exremely Fine
70-3-123B-2	Cap	ORs	Pickled copper	175.00
70-3-123B-21		Officers	PIckled copper, Wm. overlay on centre	250.00

124TH PIONEER BATTALION

No.: 70-3-124   GOVERNOR GENERAL'S BODY GUARD

The 124th Battalion was raised in Toronto, Ontario, on December 22, 1915, under the authority of G.O. 151. It was mobilized in Toronto and sailed overseas on August 9th, 1916, under the command of Lieutenant-Colonel W.C.V. Chadwick, with a strength of 32 officers and 1,004 other ranks. In England the battalion was redesignated as the 124th Pioneer Battalion. It was disbanded on September 15, 1920.

G.G.B.G. AND M.H.
CANADA OVERSEAS BN/124

Makers: Birks, Caron, Ellis, Tiptaft
Fasteners: Lugs
Composition:
  Other Ranks: Pickled copper; blackened copper or brass
  Officers: Gilt on copper
Ref.: Babin, Meek, Stewart, Cox

Note: Two makers of this cap badge exist:
  1. Ellis *(illustrated)* — pointed-leaf design with a unicorn with a split tail
  2. Tiptaft — blunt-leaf design with a unicorn with a single tail

Note: The central device of the cap was used to make the collars.

Badge No.	Insignia	Rank	Description	Extremely Fine
70-3-124-2	Cap	ORs	Pickled copper; Ellis	25.00
70-3-124-4		ORs	Blackened copper; Ellis	20.00
70-3-124-6		ORs	Blackened copper; Tiptaft	20.00
70-3-124-8		ORs	Blackened brass; Tiptaft	20.00
70-3-124-21		Officers	Gilt on copper; Ellis	65.00
70-3-124-41	Collars	ORs	Pickled copper; Ellis	16.00
70-3-124-43		ORs	Blackened copper; Ellis	16.00
70-3-124-45		ORs	Blackened brass; Tiptaft	12.00
70-3-124-61		Officers	Gilt on copper; Ellis	35.00
70-3-124-91	Shoulders	ORs	Numeral: "124;" Caron	14.00
70-3-124-93		ORS	Numeral: "124;" Birks	14.00
70-3-124-95		ORs	Numeral: "124;" Tiptaft	14.00

No.: 70-5-1

PIONEER DRAFT

OVERSEAS/CANADIAN PIONEERS

Makers: Allan
Fasteners: Lugs, tangs, pin
Composition:
Other Ranks: Pickled copper; browning copper
Officers: Browning copper
Ref.: Babin 1-6, Cox 867

Badge No.	Insignia	Rank	Description	Extremely Fine
70-5-1-2	Cap	ORs	Pickled copper; Allan	75.00
70-5-1-4		ORs	Browning copper; Allan	75.00
70-5-1-21		Officers	Browning copper, pin; Allan	100.00
70-5-1-41	Collars	ORs	Pickled copper; Allan	35.00
70-5-1-43		ORs	Browning copper; Allan	18.00
70-5-1-61		Officers	Browning copper, pin; Allan	25.00

No.: 70-7-1   **CANADIAN PIONEER TRAINING DEPOT**

CPTD

Makers: Gaunt
Fasteners: Lugs, tangs
Composition:
 Other Ranks: Browning copper
 Officers: Browning copper with silver overlay "CPTD"
Ref.: Not previously listed

Badge No.	Insignia	Rank	Description	Extremely Fine
70-7-1-2	Cap	ORs	Browning copper	1,000.00
70-7-1-21		Officers	Browning copper, silver rectangle overlay on "CPTD"	1,500.00
70-7-1-41	Collars	ORs	Browning copper	100.00
70-7-1-61		Officers	Browning copper, silver rectangle overlay on "CPTD"	150.00
70-7-1-91	Shoulders	ORs	Unknown	- -

THE CORPS OF ROYAL CANADIAN ENGINEERS • 145

CANADIAN LABOUR BATTALIONS

The duties of the four Canadian Labour Battalions were to keep roads in good repair, to dig trenches and fill up sand bags, as well as to repair bomb and shell damage. They also manhandled heavy cases of ammunition, gas cylinders and artillery shells. The 1st and 4th Labour Battalions were absorbed by the Canadian Engineers, while the 2nd and 3rd became part of the Canadian Railway Troops.

No.: 70-9-4

4TH LABOUR BATTALION

4TH/CANADA/LABOR/OMNIA/VINCIT

Makers: Unknown
Fasteners: Lugs
Composition:
Other Ranks: Browning copper with white metal overlay on design
Officers: Gilt on copper with white metal overlay on design
Ref.: Babin 2-1, Cox 868

Badge No.	Insignia	Rank	Description	Extremely Fine
70-9-4-2	Cap	ORs	Browning copper, Wm. overlay on design	85.00
70-9-4-21		Officers	Gilt on copper, Wm overlay on design	80.00
70-9-4-41	Collars	ORs	Browning copper, Wm. overlay on design	40.00
70-9-4-61		Officers	Gilt on copper, Wm overlay on design	50.00
70-9-4-91	Shoulders	ORs	Title: "4th C.L."	25.00

No.: 70-11-1   **CANADIAN LABOUR COMPANY**

This poorly manufactured badge, made of pressed copper sheeting, was possibly worn by prisoners of war and other ethnic workers.

C.L.C.

Makers: Unknown
Fasteners: Tangs
Composition:
  Other Ranks: Copper
       Officers: Unknown
Ref.: Not previously listed

Badge No.	Insignia	Rank	Description	Extremely Fine
70-11-1-2	Cap	ORs	Copper	175.00
70-11-1-21		Officers	Unknown	- -
70-11-1-41	Collars	ORs	Unknown	- -
70-11-1-61		Officers	Unknown	- -

INFANTRY WORKS COMPANIES

No.: 70-13-1

1ST INFANTRY WORKS COMPANY

INFANTRY WORKS COMPANY/CANADIAN/1

Makers: Unknown
Fasteners: Lugs
Composition:
Other Ranks: Browning copper with white metal overlay on "1"
Officers: Unknown
Ref.: Babin 41-1

Badge No.	Insignia	Rank	Description	Extremely Fine
70-13-1-2	Cap	ORs	Browning copper, Wm. overlay on "1"	900.00
70-13-1-21		Officers	Unknown	--
70-13-1-41	Collars	ORs	Browning copper, Wm. overlay on "1"	250.00
70-13-1-61		Officers	Unknown	--

148 • THE CORPS OF ROYAL CANADIAN ENGINEERS

No.: 70-13-2 **2ND INFANTRY WORKS COMPANY**

INFANTRY WORKS COMPANY/CANADIAN/2

Makers: Unknown
Fasteners: Lugs
Composition:
Other Ranks: Browning copper with white metal overlay on "2"
Officers: Unknown
Ref.: Babin 41-2

Badge No.	Insignia	Rank	Description	Extremely Fine
70-13-2-2	Cap	ORs	Browning copper, Wm. overlay on "2"	1,000.00
70-13-2-21		Officers	Unknown	- -
70-13-2-41	Collars	ORs	Browning copper, Wm. overlay on "2"	350.00
70-13-2-61		Officers	Unknown	- -

No.: 70-13-3 **3RD INFANTRY WORKS COMPANY**

INFANTRY WORKS COMPANY/CANADIAN/3

Makers: Unknown
Fasteners: Lugs
Composition:
Other Ranks: Browning copper with white metal overlay on "3"
Officers: Unknown
Ref.: Babin 41-3

Badge No.	Insignia	Rank	Description	Extremely Fine
70-13-3-2	Cap	ORs	Browning copper, Wm. overlay on "3"	1,250.00
70-13-3-21		Officers	Unknown	- -
70-13-3-41	Collars	ORs	Browning copper, Wm. overlay on "3"	350.00
70-13-3-61		Officers	Unknown	- -

No.: 70-13-4   **4TH INFANTRY WORKS COMPANY**

INFANTRY WORKS COMPANY/CANADIAN/4

Makers: Unknown
Fasteners: Lugs
Composition:
Other Ranks: Browning copper with white metal overlay on "4"
Officers: Unknown
Ref.: Babin 41-4, Cox 869

Badge No.	Insignia	Rank	Description	Extremely Fine
70-13-4-2	Cap	ORs	Browning copper, Wm. overlay on "4"	1,500.00
70-13-4-21		Officers	Unknown	- -
70-13-4-41	Collars	ORs	Browning copper, Wm. overlay on "4"	500.00
70-13-4-61		Officers	Unknown	- -

THE ROYAL CANADIAN ARMOURED CORPS

No.: 75-1-1
No. - 75-1-1A

CANADIAN TANK CORPS
GENERAL SERVICE BADGE

TANK CORPS/CANADA

Makers: Tiptaft, Unknown
Fasteners: Lugs
Composition:
Other Ranks: Blackened copper with white metal overlay on design
Officers: Unknown
Ref.: Babin 39-15, Cox 845

Note: Two makers of this cap badge exist:
1. Tiptaft — framed ribbons, course-veined leaf
2. Unknown — plain ribbons, pebble finish

Badge No.	Insignia	Rank	Description	Extremely Fine
75-1-1A-2	Cap	ORs	Blackened copper, Wm. overlay on design; Tiptaft	400.00
75-1-1A-4		ORs	Blackened copper, Wm. overlay on design; Unknown	400.00
75-1-1A-21		Officers	Unknown	- -
75-1-1A-41	Collars	ORs	Blackened copper, Wm. overlay on design; Tiptaft	150.00
75-1-1A-43		Ors	Blackened copper, Wm. overlay on design; Unknown	150.00

No. - 75-1-1B

INTERIM BADGE

CANADA

Makers: Black (1918), Unknown
Fasteners: Lugs
Composition:
  Other Ranks: Unknown
    Officers: Sterling Silver
Ref.: Not previously listed

Badge No.	Insignia	Rank	Description	Extremely Fine
75-1-1B-2	Cap	ORs	Unknown	- -
75-1-1B-21		Officers	Sterling silver; Black	1,500.00
75-1-1B-41	Collars	ORs	Unknown	- -
75-1-1B-61		Officers	Unknown	- -

152 • THE ROYAL CANADIAN ARMOURED CORPS

No. - 75-1-1C   **INTERIM BADGE**

The overlay of a tank with a barbed wire layer is possibly a British collar overlaid on a Canadian general list cap badge.

CANADA

Makers: Scully, General list
Fasteners: Lugs
Composition:
Other Ranks: Browning copper with white metal overlay on design
Officers: Unknown
Ref.: Not previously listed

Overlay Only

Badge No.	Insignia	Rank	Description	Extremely Fine
75-1-1C-2	Cap	ORs	Browning copper, Wm. overlay on design	250.00
75-1-1C-21		Officers	Unknown	- -
75-1-1C-41	Collars	ORs	Unknown	- -
75-1-1C-61		Officers	Unknown	- -

CANADIAN TANK BATTALIONS

No.: 75-3-1   **1ST TANK BATTALION**

The 1st Tank Battalion was organized on July 1, 1918, and disbanded on November 15, 1920.

1ST/TANK BATTALION/CANADA/C.E.F.

Makers: Hemsley, Tiptaft
Fasteners: Lugs, slide, pin
Composition:
 Other Ranks: Pickled brass
 Officers:
  A: Pickled brass with silver overlay on design
  B: Silver plate on brass
  C: Sterling silver
Ref.: Babin 32-1, Cox 846

Note: Two varieties of this cap badge exist:
 1. Hemsley — narrow crown with plain ribbon
 2. Tiptaft — wide crown with framed ribbon

Badge No.	Insignia	Rank	Description	Extremely Fine
75-3-1-2	Cap	ORs	Pickled brass; Hemsley	50.00
75-3-1-4		ORs	Pickled brass; Tiptaft	50.00
75-3-1-21		Officers	Pickled brass, silver overlay on design; Hemsley	200.00
75-3-1-23		Officers	Silver plate on brass; Hemsley	200.00
75-3-1-25		Officers	Sterling silver; Tiptaft	300.00
75-3-1-41	Collars	ORs	Pickled brass; Hemsley	20.00
75-3-1-43		ORs	Pickled brass; Tiptaft	20.00
75-3-1-61		Officers	Pickled brass, silver overlay on design; Hemsley	75.00
75-3-1-63		Officers	Silver plate on brass; Hemsley	75.00
75-3-1-65		Officers	Sterling silver; Tiptaft	100.00

No.: 75-3-2 ## 2ND TANK BATTALION

The 2nd Tank Batalion was organized on October 15, 1918, and disbanded on November 15, 1920.

2ND/TANK BATTALION/CANADA/C.E.F.

Photograph not available

Makers: Hemsley, Unknown
Fasteners: Lugs
Composition:
  Other Ranks: Pickled brass
  Officers: Unknown
Ref.: Babin 32-2, Cox 847

Note: The only known example of this cap badge is housed in the collection of the Royal Canadian Military Institute in Toronto.

Badge No.	Insignia	Rank	Description	Extremely Fine
75-3-2-2	Cap	ORs	Pickled brass; Hemsley	Extremely rare
75-3-2-21		Officers	Unknown	--
75-3-2-41	Collars	ORs	Pickled brass; Hemsley	Rare
75-3-2-61		Officers	Unknown	--

3RD TANK BATTALION

No.: 75-3-3

The 3rd Tank Battalion was organized on October 29, 1918, days before the armistice was signed, so it never saw active service. It was disbanded on December 2, 1918. All badges were hand made, possibly by a jeweller in Quebec, so each one is slightly different.

BATTALION/3/DE CHARS D'ASSAUT/CANADA

Makers: Unknown
Fasteners: Pin
Composition:
 Other Ranks: Unknown
  Officers: Sterling silver
Ref.: Not previously listed

Badge No.	Insignia	Rank	Description	Extremely Fine
75-3-3-2	Cap	ORs	Unknown	- -
75-3-3-21		Officers	Sterling silver	750.00
75-3-3-41	Collars	ORs	Unknown	- -
75-3-3-61		Officers	Unknown	- -

No.: 75-5-1   **CANADIAN TANK CORPS**
                              TRAINING INSTRUCTORS

CANADA

Photograph not available

Makers: Unknown
Fasteners: Unknown
Composition:
  Other Ranks: Maple leaf with brass overlay
  Officers: Unknown
Ref.: Babin 39-16

Badge No.	Insignia	Rank	Description	Extremely Fine
75-5-1-2	Cap	ORs	Maple leaf, brass overlay	Extremely rare
75-5-1-21		Officers	Unknown	- -
75-5-1-41	Collars	ORs	Unknown	- -
75-5-1-61		Officers	Unknown	- -

THE ROYAL CANADIAN ARMY CHAPLAIN CORPS

CANADIAN CHAPLAIN SERVICE

The Canadian Chaplain Service conducted Sunday services, wrote letters to the relatives of men killed in action and was charged with maintaining both military and spiritual morale.

No.: 80-1-1

GENERAL SERVICE BADGE

CROSS AND MAPLE LEAF DESIGN

CANADIAN SERVICE/CHAPLAIN

Makers: Gaunt, Tiptaft
Fasteners: Lugs, tangs
Composition:
Other Ranks: Not issued
Officers:
    A: Blackened copper
    B: Blackened brass
    C: Blackened white metal
Ref.: Babin 39-10, Cox 927

Note: Two makers of this cap badge exist:
    1. Tiptaft — heavy-veined leaf
    2. Gaunt — fine-veined leaf

Badge No.	Insignia	Rank	Description	Extremely Fine
80-1-1-21	Cap	Officers	Blackened copper; Tiptaft	135.00
80-1-1-23		Officers	Blackened brass; Gaunt	125.00
80-1-1-25		Officers	Blackened white metal; Tiptaft	125.00
80-1-1-61	Collars	Officers	Blackened copper; Tiptaft	25.00
80-1-1-63		Officers	Blackened brass; Gaunt	25.00
80-1-1-65		Officers	Blackened white metal; Tiptaft	25.00
80-1-1-91	Shoulders	Officers	Unknown	--

No. - 80-1-3　　　　　　　　**PLAIN FRAMED CROSS**

Makers: Scully, Unknown
Fasteners: Lugs, tangs
Composition:
Other Ranks: Not issued
　Officers:
　　A: Blackened brass
　　B: Blackened white metal
　　C: Blackened sterling silver
Ref.: Babin 39-10B, Cox 929

Badge No.	Insignia	Rank	Description	Extremely Fine
80-1-3-21	Cap	Officers	Blackened brass; Scully	90.00
80-1-3-23		Officers	Blackened white metal; Scully	90.00
80-1-3-25		Officers	Blackened sterling silver; Unknown	150.00
80-1-3-61	Collars	Officers	Blackened brass; Scully	50.00
80-1-3-63		Officers	Blackened white metal; Scully	50.00
80-1-3-65		Officers	Blackened sterling silver; Unknown	75.00
80-1-3-91	Shoulders	ORs	Unknown	--

THE ROYAL CANADIAN ARMY CHAPLAIN CORPS • 159

No. - 80-1-5   **MAPLE LEAVES IN THE ARMS OF A FRAMED CROSS**

Makers: Hemsley
Fasteners: Lugs, tangs
Composition:
  Other Ranks: Not issued
  Officers: Blackened brass
Ref.: Babin 39-10B, Cox 929 ??

Badge No.	Insignia	Rank	Description	Extremely Fine
80-1-5-21	Cap	Officers	Blackened brass; Hemsley	225.00
80-1-5-61	Collars	Officers	Blackened brass; Hemsley	100.00

No. - 80-1-7   **SQUARE STYLIZED CROSS**

Makers: Unknown
Fasteners: Lugs, tangs
Composition:
  Other Ranks: Not issued
  Officers: Blackened brass
Ref.: Babin 39-10a, Cox 928

Badge No.	Insignia	Rank	Description	Extremely Fine
80-1-7-21	Cap	Officers	Blackened brass, solid; Unknown	75.00
80-1-7-23		Officers	Blackened brass, void; Unknown	100.00
80-1-7-61	Collars	Officers	Blackened brass, solid; Unknown	50.00
80-1-7-63		Officers	Blackened brass, void; Unknown	50.00
80-1-7-91	Shoulders	ORs	Unknown	--

THE ROYAL CANADIAN ARMY CHAPLAIN CORPS

No.: 80-3-1 **SALVATION ARMY CHAPLAIN SERVICE**

BLOOD AND FIRE DESIGN
WITH RIBBON

BLOOD AND FIRE/THE SALVATION ARMY

Makers: Unknown
Fasteners: Tangs
Composition:
  Other Ranks: White metal
  Officers: Unknown
Ref.: Babin 42-9, Cox 933

Badge No.	Insignia	Rank	Description	Extremely Fine
80-3-1-2	Cap	ORs	White metal	25.00
80-3-1-21		Officers	Unknown	- -
80-3-1-41	Collars	ORs	White metal	25.00
80-3-1-61		Officers	Unknown	- -
80-3-1-91	Shoulders	ORs	Unknown	- -

No. - 80-3-3 **BLOOD AND FIRE DESIGN
WITHOUT RIBBON**

BLOOD AND FIRE

Makers: Unknown
Fasteners: Tangs
Composition:
  Other Ranks: Silverplate on white metal
  Officers: Gilt on white metal
Ref.: Babin 42-10, Cox 932

Badge No.	Insignia	Rank	Description	Extremely Fine
80-3-3-2	Cap	ORs	Silverplate on white metal	45.00
80-3-3-21		Officers	Gilt on white metal	45.00
80-3-3-41	Collars	ORs	Silverplate on white metal	20.00
80-3-3-61		Officers	Gilt on white metal	20.00
80-3-3-91	Shoulders	ORs	Unknown	- -

THE ROYAL CANADIAN ARMY MEDICAL CORPS

CANADIAN ARMY MEDICAL CORPS

The Canadian Army Medical Corps, already part of Canada's small regular force and the non-permanent active militia at the start of the war, was part of the vanguard of troops that went overseas and among the first to enter into battle. The corps was instrumental in innoculating the entire Canadian force against typhoid fever. It employed 1,351 medical officers, 1,886 nursing sisters and 12,243 field medics and orderlies.

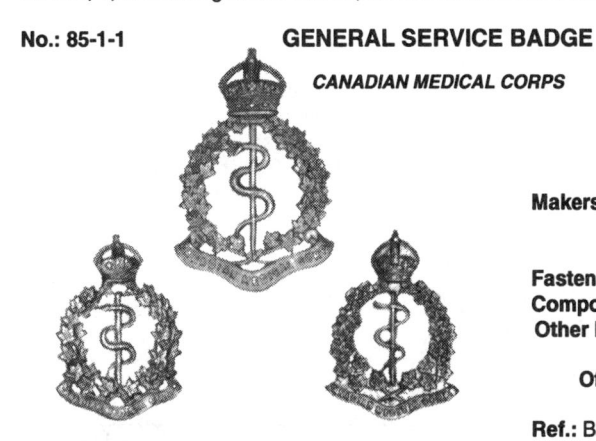

No.: 85-1-1 **GENERAL SERVICE BADGE**

CANADIAN MEDICAL CORPS

Makers: Caron, Ellis, Gaunt, Hemsley, Inglis, Roden, Tiptaft
Fasteners: Lugs, tangs
Composition:
Other Ranks: Pickled copper; browning copper
Officers: Silver with gilt on centre
Ref.: Babin 39-11, Cox 907 and 908

Badge No.	Insignia	Rank	Description	Extremely Fine
85-1-1-2	Cap	ORs	Pickled copper; Hemsley, Inglis	10.00
85-1-1-4		ORs	Pickled copper; Roden	10.00
85-1-1-6		ORs	Browning copper; Caron	10.00
85-1-1-8		ORs	Browning copper; Tiptaft	10.00
85-1-1-10		ORs	Browning copper; Gaunt	10.00
85-1-1-12		ORs	Browning copper; Ellis	10.00
85-1-1-21		Officers	Silver, gilt on centre; Caron	20.00
85-1-1-41	Collars	ORs	Pickled copper; Hemsley, Inglis	10.00
85-1-1-43		ORs	Pickled copper; Roden	10.00
85-1-1-45		ORs	Browning copper; Caron	10.00
85-1-1-47		ORs	Browning copper; Tiptaft	10.00
85-1-1-49		ORs	Browning copper; Gaunt	10.00
85-1-1-51		ORs	Browning copper; Ellis	10.00
85-1-1-61		Officers	Silver, gilt on centre; Caron	15.00
85-1-1-91	Shoulders	ORs	Title: "CAMC;" Hemsley, Inglis	15.00
85-1-1-93		ORs	Title: "CAMC;" Roden	15.00
85-1-1-95		ORs	Title" "CAMC;" Ellis	15.00

CANADIAN STATIONARY HOSPITALS

In 1918 there were six Canadian stationary hospitals in France, numbers 1, 2, 3, 7, 8, 9 and 10. It appears that only two, numbers 8 and 9, had distinctive badges. Possibly the others wore the Medical Corps general service badge.

No.: 85-3-8

8TH STATIONARY HOSPITAL

8/STATIONARY HOSPITAL/SASKATCHEWAN/ OVERSEAS/CANADA

Makers: Hemsley
Fasteners: Lugs
Composition:
  Other Ranks: Pickled copper
  Officers: Unknown
Ref.: Babin 27-8, Cox 913

Badge No.	Insignia	Rank	Description	Extremely Fine
85-3-8-2	Cap	ORs	Pickled copper; Hemsley	200.00
85-3-8-21		Officers	Unknown	- -
85-3-8-41	Collars	ORs	Pickled copper; Hemsley	35.00
85-3-8-61		Officers	Unknown	- -
85-3-8-91	Shoulders	ORs	Unknown	- -

9TH STATIONARY HOSPITAL

No.: 85-3-9

The 9th Stationary Hospital was organized on July 15, 1916, and disbanded on November 15, 1920.

ST. F.X. OVERSEAS STY. HOSP./9/C.A.M.C.

Makers: Hemsley
Fasteners: Lugs
Composition:
  Other Ranks: Pickled copper
  Officers: Silver
Ref.: Babin 27-9, Cox 914

Badge No.	Insignia	Rank	Description	Extremely Fine
85-3-9-2	Cap	ORs	Pickled copper; Hemsley	375.00
85-3-9-21		Officers	Silver; Hemsley	400.00
85-3-9-41	Collars	ORs	Pickled copper; Hemsley	75.00
85-3-9-61		Officers	Silver; Hemsley	100.00
85-3-9-91	Shoulders	ORs	Unknown	--

CANADIAN CASUALTY CLEARING STATIONS

There were four Canadian casualty clearing stations, one for each division, but only the 2nd had its own insignia.

No.: 85-5-2   2ND CASUALTY CLEARING STATION

The 2nd Casualty Clearing Statin was organized on March 15, 1915. It is presumed that the staff wore the C.A.M.C. general service cap and collar badges with the 2nd Casualty Clearing Station shoulder title. It was disbanded on November 1, 1920.

SHOULDER TITLE ONLY

2/CCS/CANADA

Makers: Unknown
Fasteners: Lugs
Composition:
   Other Ranks: Unknown
   Officers: Unknown
Ref.: Not previously listed

Badge No.	Insignia	Rank	Description	Extremely Fine
85-5-2-91	Shoulders	ORs	Title: "2/CCS/CANADA;" Unknown	100.00

CANADIAN FIELD AMBULANCES

By 1918 there were 14 Canadian field ambulances in operation in France.

No.: 85-7-1   **1ST CANADIAN FIELD AMBULANCE**

The 1st Canadian Field Ambulance was organized on August 6, 1914, and disbanded on November 15, 1920.

The Canadian Medical Corps General Service Badge was modified by removing the centre device and adding "1st CAN FLD AMB."

1ST/CAN/FLD/AMB/CANADIAN MEDICAL CORPS

Makers: Unknown
Fasteners: Lugs
Composition:
  Other Ranks: Pickled copper
  Officers: Gilt on copper
Ref.: Babin 26-1

Badge No.	Insignia	Rank	Description	Extremely Fine
85-7-1-2	Cap	ORs	Pickled copper; Unknown	500.00
85-7-1-21		Officers	Gilt on copper	850.00
85-7-1-41	Collars	ORs	Unknown	--
85-7-1-61		Officers	Unknown	--
85-7-1-91	Shoulders	ORs	Title: "1ST CANADIAN/FLD.AMB.;" Unknown	15.00
85-7-1-93		ORs	Title: "AMB"	10.00

No.: 85-7-2A   2ND CANADIAN FIELD AMBULANCE

The 2nd Canadian Field Ambulance was organized on August 6, 1914, and disbanded on November 15, 1920.

WITHOUT "OVERSEAS"

QUEEN'S UNIVERSITY/FIELD AMBULANCE

Makers: Unknown
Fasteners: Lugs
Composition:
  Other Ranks: Pickled brass
  Officers: Unknown
Ref.: Babin 26-9, Cox 912

Badge No.	Insignia	Rank	Description	Extremely Fine
85-7-2A-2	Cap	ORs	Pickled brass; Unknown	140.00
85-7-2A-21		Officers	Unknown	- -
85-7-2A-41	Collars	ORs	Pickled brass; Unknown	35.00
85-7-2A-61		Officers	Unknown	- -
85-7-2A-91	Shoulders	ORs	Unknown	- -

No. - 85-7-2B WITH "OVERSEAS"

QUEEN'S UNIVERSITY/FIELD AMBULANCE/OVERSEAS

Makers: Unknown
Fasteners: Lugs
Composition:
 Other Ranks: Pickled brass
  Officers: Unknown
Ref.: Not previously listed

Badge No.	Insignia	Rank	Description	Extremely Fine
85-7-2B-2	Cap	ORs	Pickled brass; Unknown	150.00
85-7-2B-2		Officers	Unknown	- -
85-7-2B-41	Collars	ORs	Pickled brass; Unknown	25.00
85-7-2B-61		Officers	Unknown	- -
85-7-2B-91	Shoulders	ORs	Unknown	- -

No. - 85-7-2C

INTERIM BADGE

2/AMB/CANADA

Makers: General list
Fasteners: Lugs
Composition:
 Other Ranks: Brass overlay
     Officers: Unknown
Ref.: Not previously listed

Badge No.	Insignia	Rank	Description	Extremely Fine
85-7-2C-2	Cap	ORs	General list, brass overlay on "2/AMB"	450.00
85-7-2C-21		Officers	Unknown	- -
85-7-2C-41	Collars	ORs	General list, brass overlay on "2/AMB"	150.00
85-7-2C-61		Officers	Unknown	- -
85-7-1C-91	Shoulders	ORs	Title: "2/AMB"	50.00

THE ROYAL CANADIAN ARMY MEDICAL CORPS • 169

No.: 85-7-3   **3RD CANADIAN FIELD AMBULANCE**

The 3rd Canadian Field Ambulance was organized on August 6, 1914. It is assumed that the staff members wore the universal C.A.M.C. cap and collar badges with the 3rd title on them. The unit was disbanded on November 15, 1920.

SHOULDER TITLE ONLY

FIELD AMB/THIRD/CANADA

Makers: Tiptaft
Fasteners: Lugs
Composition:
  Other Ranks: Copper
  Officers: Unknown
Ref.: Not previously listed

Badge No.	Insignia	Rank	Description	Extremely Fine
85-7-3-91	Shoulders	ORs	Title: "FIELD AMB/THIRD/CANADA"	125.00

No.: 85-7-4   **4TH CANADIAN FIELD AMBULANCE**

N ARDUIS FIDELIS/4/CANADIAN FIELD AMBULANCE/2 DIV

Makers: Unknown
Fasteners: Lugs
Composition:
  Other Ranks: Blackened copper or brass
  Officers: Unknown
Ref.: Babin 26-4, Cox 909

Badge No.	Insignia	Rank	Description	Extremely Fine
85-7-4-2	Cap	ORs	Blackened copper; Unknown	400.00
85-7-4-4		ORs	Blackened brass; Unknown	500.00
85-7-4-21		Officers	Unknown	--
85-7-4-41	Collars	ORs	Blackened copper; Unknown	75.00
85-7-4-43		ORs	Blackened brass; Unknown	75.00
85-7-4-61		Officers	Unknown	--
85-7-4-91	Shoulders	ORs	Title: "CAN (CAMC BADGE) ADA 4TH FIELD AMBULANCE;" Unknown	50.00

No.: 85-7-8   8TH CANADIAN FIELD AMBULANCE

CANADIAN/8/FIELD AMBULANCE

Makers: Unknown
Fasteners: Lugs
Composition:
  Other Ranks: Pickled copper or brass
  Officers: Unknown
Ref.: Babin 26-8, Cox 911

Badge No.	Insignia	Rank	Description	Extremely Fine
85-7-8-2	Cap	ORs	Pickled copper; Unknown	400.00
85-7-8-4		ORs	Pickled brass; Unknown	250.00
85-7-8-21		Officers	Unknown	- -
85-7-8-41	Collars	ORs	Pickled copper; Unknown	125.00
85-7-8-43		ORs	Pickled brass; Unknown	100.00
85-7-8-61		Officers	Unknown	- -
85-7-8-91	Shoulders	ORs	Title: "FLD AMB/CAN 8 ADA"	50.00

No.: 85-7-9   9TH CANADIAN FIELD AMBULANCE

AMB/9/CANADA

Makers: Birks
Fasteners: Lugs, tangs
Composition:
  Other Ranks: Pickled brass
  Officers: Unknown
Ref.: Not previously listed

Badge No.	Insignia	Rank	Description	Extremely Fine
85-7-9-2	Cap	ORs	Pickled brass; Birks	200.00
85-7-9-21		Officers	Unknown	- -
85-7-9-41	Collars	ORs	Unknown	- -
85-7-9-61		Officers	Unknown	- -

No.: 85-7-10   10TH CANADIAN FIELD AMBULANCE

It is presumed that the 10th Canadian Field Ambulance wore the C.A.M.C. cap and collar badges in conjunction with the 10th Canadian Field Ambulance shoulder titles.

SHOULDER TITLES ONLY

10 FIELD AMBULANCE/CAMC/CANADA

Makers: Inglis, Tiptaft
Fasteners: Lugs
Composition:
 Other Ranks: General service
 Officers: General service
Ref.: Not previoulsy listed

Badge No.	Insignia	Rank	Description	Extremely Fine
85-7-10-91	Shoulders	ORs	Title: "10 FIELD AMBULANCE/CAMC/CANADA;" Inglis	75.00
85-7-10-93		ORs	Title: "10 FIELD AMBULANCE/CAMC/CANADA;" Tiptaft	40.00

THE ROYAL CANADIAN ARMY PAY CORPS

CANADIAN ARMY PAY CORPS

The Canadian Army Pay Corps (Overseas) was organized on August 6, 1914, to pay the troops and maintain important records. They were an arm of the Corps Troops serving throughout the Canadian Expeditionary Force and the Canadian Siberian Expeditionary Force. It was disbanded on November 15, 1920.

No.: 90-1-1

GENERAL SERVICE BADGES
SINGLE MAPLE LEAF DESIGN
C.A.P.C.

Makers: Ellis, Gaunt, Hemsley, Tiptaft
Fasteners: Pin, lugs, tangs
Composition:
Other Ranks: Browning copper or brass
Officers:
   A: Gilt on brass
   B: Silver and gilt
Ref.: Babin 39-5, Cox 934

Note: Three varieties of this cap badge exist:
  1. Hemsley — thick-necked beaver, heavy-veined leaf
  2. Ellis — thin-necked beaver, fine-veined leaf
  3. Gaunt — snarling beaver, fine-veined leaf

Badge No.	Insignia	Rank	Description	Extremely Fine
90-1-1-2	Cap	ORs	Browning copper; Hemsley	20.00
90-1-1-4		ORs	Browning copper; Tiptaft	20.00
90-1-1-6		ORs	Browning brass; Gaunt	20.00
90-1-1-21		Officers	Gilt on brass; Ellis	75.00
90-1-1-23		Officers	Silver and gilt; Gaunt	75.00
90-1-1-41	Collars	ORs	Browning copper; Hemsley	35.00
90-1-1-43		ORs	Browning copper; Tiptaft	35.00
90-1-1-45		ORs	Browning brass; Gaunt	40.00
90-1-1-61		Officers	Gilt on brass; Ellis	50.00
90-1-1-63		Officers	Silver and gilt; Gaunt	50.00
90-1-1-91	Shoulders	ORs	Title: "C.A.P.C."	10.00

THE ROYAL CANADIAN ARMY PAY CORPS • 173

No. - 90-1-3

SIX MAPLE LEAVES DESIGN

C.A.P.C./OVERSEAS

Makers: Gaunt, Tiptaft
Fasteners: Lugs
Composition:
 Other Ranks: Browning copper
  Officers: Browning copper
Ref.: Babin 39-5A, Cox 935

Badge No.	Insignia	Rank	Description	Extremely Fine
90-1-3-2	Cap	ORs	Browning copper; Tiptaft	15.00
90-1-3-4		ORs	Browning copper; Gaunt	15.00
90-1-3-21		Officers	Browning copper; Gaunt	50.00
90-1-3-41	Collars	ORs	Browning copper; Tiptaft	40.00
90-1-3-43		ORs	Browning copper; Gaunt	40.00
90-1-3-61		Officers	Browning copper; Gaunt	40.00

THE ROYAL CANADIAN ARMY SERVICE CORPS

CANADIAN ARMY SERVICE CORPS

The Canadian Army Service Corps was charged with supplying the forces with transportation, food and workshops.

No.: 95-1-1 **GENERAL SERVICE BADGE**

CANADIAN ARMY SERVICE CORPS

Makers: Birks, Dingwall, Hemsley, Inglis, Roden, Scully, Tiptaft
Fasteners: Lugs
Composition:
Other Ranks: Pickled copper or brass; browning copper
Officers: Silver with gilt overlay on design
Ref.: Babin 19-1, Cox 896

Note: Over eight different makers are known, but all are not listed. Also, most of the badges were issued with either a solid or a void field.

Badge No.	Insignia	Rank	Description	Extremely Fine
95-1-1-2	Cap	ORs	Pickled copper; Hemsley	10.00
95-1-1-4		ORs	Pickled brass; Inglis	10.00
95-1-1-6		ORs	Browning copper; Birks	10.00
95-1-1-21		Officers	Silver, gilt overlay on design; Hemsley	100.00
95-1-1-41	Collars	ORs	Pickled copper; Hemsley	12.00
95-1-1-43		ORs	Pickled brass; Inglis	12.00
95-1-1-45		ORs	Browning copper; Birks	12.00
95-1-1-61		Officers	Silver, gilt overlay on design; Hemsley	50.00
95-1-1-91	Shoulders	ORs	Title: "CASC;" Scully	10.00
95-1-1-93		ORs	Title: "CASC;" Roden	10.00
95-1-1-95		ORs	Title: "CASC;" Tiptaft	10.00
95-1-1-97		ORs	Title: "CASC;" Greatcoat	20.00
95-1-1-99		ORs	Title: "CANADA/OVERSEAS;" Dingwall	12.00
95-1-1-101		ORs	Title: "CANADA/OVERSEAS;" Hemsley	12.00

ARMY SERVICES COMPANIES

No.: 95-3-7

7TH COMPANY
CANADA/7 CO CASC WINNIPEG

Makers: Unknown
Fasteners: Lugs
Composition:
  Other Ranks: Browning copper
  Officers: Unknown
Ref.: Not previously listed

Badge No.	Insignia	Rank	Description	Extremely Fine
95-3-7-2	Cap	ORs	Browning copper	Rare
95-3-7-21		Officers	Unknown	- -
95-3-7-41	Collars	ORs	Browning copper	Rare
95-3-7-61		Officers	Unknown	- -
95-3-7-91	Shoulders	ORs	Unknown	- -

No.: 95-3-19

19TH COMPANY
SHOULDER TITLE ONLY

19/CASC

Photograph not available

Makers: Unknown
Fasteners: Lugs
Composition:
  Other Ranks: Copper
  Officers: Unknown
Ref.: Not previously listed

Badge No.	Insignia	Rank	Description	Extremely Fine
95-3-19-91	Shoulders	ORs	Title: "19/CASC"	20.00

AMMUNITION SUB PARK COMPANIES

No.: 95-5-1 **1ST AMMUNITION SUB PARK**

The 1st Ammunition Sub Park was organized on March 15, 1915, and disbanded on November 1, 1920.

1/A.S.P/CANADA

Makers: Gaunt, Unknown
Fasteners: Lugs
Composition:
  Other Ranks: Blackened brass
  Officers: Unknown
Ref.: Babin 18-1, Cox 427

Badge No.	Insignia	Rank	Description	Extremely Fine
95-5-1-2	Cap	ORs	Blackened brass; Gaunt	250.00
95-5-1-21		Officers	Unknown	--
95-5-1-41	Collars	ORs	Blackened brass; Gaunt	75.00
95-5-1-61		Officers	Unknown	--
95-5-1-91	Shoulders	ORs	Unknown	--

No.: 95-5-2 **2ND AMMUNITION SUB PARK**

The 2nd Ammunition Sub Park was organized on March 15, 1915, and disbanded on November 1, 1920.

2/A.S.P/CANADA

Makers: Gaunt, Unknown
Fasteners: Lugs
Composition:
  Other Ranks: Blackened brass
  Officers: Unknown
Ref.: Babin 18-2, Cox 428

Badge No.	Insignia	Rank	Description	Extremely Fine
95-5-2-2	Cap	ORs	Blackened brass; Gaunt	400.00
95-5-2-21		Officers	Unknown	--
95-5-2-41	Collars	ORs	Blackened brass; Gaunt	125.00
95-5-2-61		Officers	Unknown	--
95-5-2-91	Shoulders	ORs	Unknown	--

THE ROYAL CANADIAN ARMY SERVICE CORPS • 177

No.: 95-5-3   **3RD AMMUNITION SUB PARK**

The 3rd Ammunition Sub Park was organized on July 15, 1916, and disbanded on November 1, 1920.

3/A.S.P/CANADA

Makers: Gaunt, Unknown
Fasteners: Lugs
Composition:
Other Ranks: Blackened brass
     Officers: Unknown
Ref.: Babin 18-3, Cox 429

Badge No.	Insignia	Rank	Description	Extremely Fine
95-5-3-2	Cap	ORs	Blackened brass; Gaunt	250.00
95-5-3-21		Officers	Unknown	- -
95-5-3-41	Collars	ORs	Blackened brass; Gaunt	75.00
95-5-3-61		Officers	Unknown	- -
95-5-3-91	Shoulders	ORs	Unknown	- -

No.: 95-5-4   **4TH AMMUNITION SUB PARK**

The 4th Ammunution Sub Park was organized on July 15, 1916, and disbanded on November 1, 1920.

4/A.S.P/CANADA

Makers: Gaunt, Unknown
Fasteners: Lugs
Composition:
Other Ranks: Blackened brass
     Officers: Unknown
Ref.: Babin 18-4, Cox 430

Badge No.	Insignia	Rank	Description	Extremely Fine
95-5-4-2	Cap	ORs	Blackened brass; Gaunt	275.00
95-5-4-21		Officers	Unknown	- -
95-5-4-41	Collars	ORs	Blackened brass; Gaunt	75.00
95-5-4-61		Officers	Unknown	- -
95-5-4-91	Shoulders	ORs	Unknown	- -

DIVISIONAL TRAINS

No.: 95-7-4   **4TH TRAIN**

The 4th Train was organized on July 15, 1916, and disbanded on November 1, 1920.

CANADIAN ARMY SERVICE CORPS OVERSEAS/
4TH/DIVISIONAL TRAIN

Makers: Hemsley
Fasteners: Lugs
Composition:
  Other Ranks: Pickled copper
  Officers: Pickled copper with silver overlay on design
Ref.: Babin 19-3, Cox 897

Badge No.	Insignia	Rank	Description	Extremely Fine
95-7-4-2	Cap	ORs	Pickled copper; Hemsley	50.00
95-7-4-21		Officers	Pickled copper, silver overlay on design	200.00
95-7-4-41	Collars	ORs	Pickled copper; Hemsley	25.00
95-7-4-61		Officers	Pickled copper, silver overlay on design	75.00
95-7-4-91	Shoulders	ORs	Title: "C.A.S.C. OVERSEAS/CANADA/ FOURTH DIVISIONAL TRAIN"	30.00

No.: 95-9-1

AMMUNITION SUB PARK MECHANICAL TRANSPORT COMPANY

ASP/CANADIAN EXPEDITIONARY FORCE/MT/CANADA

Makers: Ellis
Fasteners: Lugs
Composition:
  Other Ranks: Blackened brass
      Officers:
         A: Silver
         B: Browning copper
Ref.: Babin 18-5, Cox 431

Badge No.	Insignia	Rank	Description	Extremely Fine
95-9-1-2	Cap	ORs	Blackened brass; Ellis	250.00
95-9-1-21		Officers	Silver; Ellis	400.00
		Maple Leaf Design		
95-9-1-41	Collars	ORs	Blackened brass; Ellis	50.00
95-9-1-61		Officers	Silver; Ellis	100.00
		Truck Design		
95-9-1-43	Collars	ORs	Unknown	- -
95-9-1-63		Officers	Browning copper; Ellis	100.00
95-9-1-91	Shoulders	ORs	Title: "MT," Small	15.00
95-9-1-93		ORs	Title: "MT," Large	20.00
95-9-1-95		ORs	Title: "CAN (BADGE) ADA"	35.00

No.: 95-11-4   **4TH AMBULANCE WORKSHOP**

Only a collar is known at this time.

CANADIAN ARMY SERVICE CORPS

OVERSEAS/4TH/AMULANCE/WORKSHOP

Photograph not available

Makers: Hemsley, Unknown
Fasteners: Lugs
Composition:
  Other Ranks: Pickled copper
  Officers: Unknown
Ref.: Not previously listed

Badge No.	Insignia	Rank	Description	Extremely Fine
95-11-4-2	Cap	ORs	Unknown	--
95-11-4-21		Officers	Unknown	--
95-11-4-41	Collars	ORs	Pickled copper; Hemlsey	Rare
95-11-4-61		Officers	Unknown	--

ARMY SERVICE DEPOT COMPANIES

No.: 95-13-8   8TH (OVERSEAS) DEPOT UNIT OF SUPPLY

The 8th (Overseas) Depot Unit of Supply was organized on December 22, 1915, and disbanded on November 1, 1920.

ASC-CEF/8/CANADA

Makers: Jacoby, Unknown
Fasteners: Pins, lugs
Composition:
  Other Ranks: Gilt on copper
  Officers: Unknown
Ref.: Babin 19-4, Cox 898

Badge No.	Insignia	Rank	Description	Extremely Fine
95-13-8-2	Cap	ORs	Gilt on copper; Jacoby	50.00
95-13-8-21		Officers	Unknown	--
95-13-8-41	Collars	ORs	Unknown	--
95-13-8-61		Officers	Unknown	--
95-13-8-91	Shoulders	ORs	Title: "8/ASC"	25.00

182 • THE ROYAL CANADIAN ARMY SERVICE CORPS

No.: 95-13-21   21ST (OVERSEAS) DEPOT UNIT OF SUPPLY

It is presumed that the 21st Depot wore the Canadian Army Service Corps general service cap and collar badges along with the 21st shoulder title.

SHOULDER TITLE ONLY

21 C.A.S.C.

Makers: Unknown
Fasteners: Lugs
Composition:
 Other Ranks: Copper
  Officers: Unknown
Ref.: Not previously listed

Badge No.	Insignia	Rank	Description	Extremely Fine
95-13-21-91	Shoulders	ORs	Title: "21 CASC"	30.00

No.: 95-15-1   REMOUNT DEPOT

The Remount Depot was organized on July 1, 1915, and disbanded on November 1, 1920.

REMOUNT DEPOT C.E.F./CANADA

Makers: Hemsley, Inglis, Unknown
Fasteners: Lugs
Composition:
 Other Ranks: Pickled copper; browning copper
  Officers: Unknown
Ref.: Babin 11-1, Cox 435

Badge No.	Insignia	Rank	Description	Extremely Fine
95-15-1-2	Cap	ORs	Pickled copper; Hemsley, Inglis	50.00
95-15-1-4		ORs	Browning copper; Hemsley, Inglis	75.00
95-15-1-21		Officers	Unknown	- -
95-15-1-41	Collars	ORs	Pickled copper; Hemsley, Inglis	30.00
95-15-1-43		ORs	Browning copper; Hemsley, Inglis	50.00
95-15-1-61		Officers	Unknown	- -
95-15-1-91	Shoulders	ORs	Unknown	- -

TRAINING DEPOTS

No.: 95-17-1 **1ST OVERSEAS TRAINING DEPOT**

The 1st Overseas Training Depot was organized on July 15, 1915, and disbanded on November 1, 1920.

CASC/OVERSEAS NO.1 TRAINING/DEPOT/CANADA

Makers: Dingwall
Fasteners: Lugs, tangs
Composition:
Other Ranks: Pickled brass; Blackened copper
Officers:
  A: Pickled brass with silver overlay and blue enamel
  B: Pickled brass with blue and white enamelled centre
Ref.: Babin 19-2, Cox 899

Badge No.	Insignia	Rank	Description	Extremely Fine
95-17-1-2	Cap	ORs	Pickled brass; Dingwall	50.00
95-17-1-4		ORs	Blackened copper; Dingwall	50.00
95-17-1-21		Officers	Pickled brass, silver overlay and blue enamelled centre	150.00
95-17-1-23		Officers	Pickled brass, blue and white enamelled centre	150.00
95-17-1-41	Collars	ORs	Pickled brass; Dingwall	60.00
95-17-1-43		ORs	Blackened copper; Dingwall	60.00
95-17-1-61		Officers	Pickled brass, silver overlay and blue enamelled centre	75.00
95-17-1-63		Officers	Pickled brass, blue and white enamelled centre	75.00
95-17-1-91	Shoulders	ORs	Title: "CAN (CASC BADGE) ADA/ OVER-SEAS"	30.00

THE ROYAL CANADIAN CORPS OF SIGNALS

CANADIAN SIGNAL CORPS

Although the Canadian Signal Corps had its own headquarters, it operated as an integral part of the Canadian Engineers in providing equipment and developing and maintaining vital communications links.

No.: 100-1-1   **GENERAL SERVICE BADGE**

CYPHER "CSC"/VELOX VERSUTOS VICILANS

Makers: Ellis, Scully, Unknown
Fasteners: Lugs
Composition:
  Other Ranks: Copper; brass
  Officers: Gilt on brass enamelled
Ref.: Small; Babin 33-1, Cox 859
     Large; Babin 33-2, Cox 860

Small Cap   Large Cap

Small Collar   Large Collar

Note: Two different makers of this cap badge exist:
1. Unknown — large badge, 43 mm x 43 mm
2. Ellis — small badge, 43 mm x 32 mm

Badge No.	Insignia	Rank	Description	Extremely Fine
100-1-1-2	Cap	ORs	Copper, large; Unknown	45.00
100-1-1-4		ORs	Brass, large; Unknown	45.00
100-1-1-6		ORs	Copper, small; Ellis	45.00
100-1-1-8		ORs	Brass, small; Ellis	45.00
100-1-1-21		Officers	Gilt on brass, enamelled	300.00
100-1-1-41	Collars	ORs	Copper	40.00
100-1-1-43		ORs	Brass	40.00
100-1-1-61		Officers	Gilt on brass, enamelled	100.00
100-1-1-91	Shoulders	ORs	Title: "CCOFS;" Scully	20.00
100-1-1-93		ORs	Title: "CANADIAN/SIGNAL CORPS"	20.00
100-1-1-95		ORs	Title: "SIGNAL"	15.00
100-1-1-97		ORs	Title: "C.S.C."	15.00

THE ROYAL CANADIAN DENTAL CORPS

CANADIAN ARMY DENTAL CORPS

The medical standards of the Canadian Army were very rigid and numerous recruits were turned away due to poor teeth. In 1915 the Canadian Dental Association approached Sir Samuel Hughes, Minister of Militia, offering to establish a dental corps within the army to remedy this situation. It is believed that the Canadian Army Dental Corps was the first corps of its kind. The first draft consisted of some 27 officers, all dental surgeons, 35 N.C.O.s, who were dental technicians, and 40 privates. It is estimated that nearly 2.5 million dental procedures were performed during the war in England and France alone. At the war's end, every returning soldier was given dental treatment.

No.: 105-1-1   **GENERAL SERVICE BADGE**

No. - 105-1-1A   **ERROR LEGEND — DS FOR DENTAL SERVICE**

CANADIAN/ARMY DENTAL CORPS (DS)

Makers: Birks, Caron, Hemsley, Unknown
Fasteners: Lugs
Composition:
  Other Ranks: Pickled copper or brass
  Officers: Unknown
Ref.: Babin 39-7, Cox 904

Badge No.	Insignia	Rank	Description	Extremely Fine
105-1-1A-2	Cap	ORs	Pickled copper; Hemsley	22.00
105-1-1A-4		ORs	Pickled brass; Hemsley	16.00
105-1-1A-21		Officers	Unknown	--
105-1-1A-41	Collars	ORs	Pickled copper; Hemsley	15.00
105-1-1A-43		ORs	Pickled brass; Hemsley	15.00
105-1-1A-61		Officers	Unknown	--
105-1-1A-91	Shoulders	ORs	Title: "C.A.D.C.;" Birks	10.00
105-1-1A-93		ORs	Title: "C.A.D.C.;" Caron	10.00
105-1-1A-95		ORs	Title: "C.A.D.C.;" Unknown	10.00

No. - 105-1-1B   **CORRECTED LEGEND — OS FOR OVERSEAS**

CANADIAN/ARMY DENTAL CORPS (OS)

Makers: Birks, Tiptaft, Unknown
Fasteners: Lugs
Composition:
Other Ranks: Pickled brass; browning copper
Officers: Gilt on brass
Ref.: Babin 39-8, Cox 905

Small Cap   Large Cap

Note: Three makers of this cap badge exist:
1. Birks — Narrow, small fine-veined leaf, small cap, 40 mm
2. Tiptaft — Wide, large course-veined leaf, large cap, 45 mm
3. Unknown

Badge No.	Insignia	Rank	Description	Extremely Fine
105-1-1B-2	Cap	ORs	Pickled brass; Birks	30.00
105-1-1B-4		ORs	Browning copper; Tiptaft	30.00
105-1-1B-6		ORs	Browning copper; Unknown	30.00
105-1-1B-21		Officers	Gilt on brass; Birks	50.00
105-1-1B-41	Collars	ORs	Pickled brass; Birks	22.00
105-1-1B-43		ORs	Browning copper, Tiptaft	22.00
105-1-1B-45		ORs	Browning copper; Unknown	22.00
105-1-1B-61		Officers	Gilt on brass; Birks	30.00

No. - 105-1-3

"CADC" CYPHER DESIGN

CADC

Makers: G & S Co., Unknown
Fasteners: Lugs, tangs
Composition:
 Other Ranks: Browning copper or brass
 Officers: Unknown
Ref.: Babin 39-8, Cox 906

Badge No.	Insignia	Rank	Description	Extremely Fine
105-1-3-2	Cap	ORs	Browning copper; G & S Co.	30.00
105-1-3-4		ORs	Browning copper; Unknown	30.00
105-1-3-6		ORs	Browning brass; Unknown	30.00
105-1-3-21		Officers	Unknown	- -
105-1-3-41	Collars	ORs	Browning copper; G & S C0.	20.00
105-1-3-43		ORs	Browning copper; Unknown	20.00
105-1-3-45		ORs	Browning brass; Unknown	20.00
105-1-3-61		Officers	Unknown	- -

THE ROYAL CANADIAN HORSE ARTILLERY

The Royal Canadian Horse Artillery was organized on August 6, 1914. Lieutenant-Colonel Andrew McNaughton, D.S.O., advanced the science of artillery through the development of the "rolling barrage", whereby advancing infantry would follow as close as 30 yards behind their own exploding shells, thus diminishing the ability of the enemy to identify non-protected areas of the assault. He also devised a system of "indirect fire" which allowed protection to the flanks of the advancing infantry by means of a protective web of bursting shells.

The total strength of the Royal Canadian Horse Artillery was 37,714 all ranks, with casualties numbering 9,984 by the end of the conflict. It was disbanded on November 1, 1920.

No.: 110-1-1   **GENERAL SERVICE BADGE**

ROYAL CANADIAN ARTILLERY/GVR

Makers: Hemsley, Roden
Fasteners: Lugs, Tangs

Composition:
Other Ranks: Browning copper
Officers: Browning copper; superior construction
Ref.: Babin 16-2, Cox 329 and 330 Mazeus MS-11

Badge No.	Insignia	Rank	Description	Extremely Fine
110-1-1-2	Cap	ORs	Browning copper; Roden	50.00
110-1-1-4		ORs	Browning copper; Hemsley	50.00
110-1-1-21		Officers	Browning copper; Hemsley	75.00
110-1-1-41	Collars	ORs	Browning copper; Hemsley	Rare
110-1-1-61		Officers	Browning copper; Hemsley	Rare
110-1-1-91	Shoulders	ORs	Title: "R.C.H.A."	16.00

THE ROYAL CANADIAN ORDNANCE CORPS

CANADIAN ORDNANCE CORPS

The Royal Canadian Ordnance Corps had the task of supplying, equipping and outfitting the entire Canadian Corps.

The insignia was produced over a long period of time by many makers. The badges worn by the Corp in World War 1 originated prior to this period.

No.: 125-1-1   **GENERAL SERVICE BADGE**

ORDNANCE

Makers: Caron, Hemsley, Hicks, Gaunt, Tiptaft, Unknown
Fasteners: Lugs
Composition:
 Other Ranks: Copper; brass
 Officers:
  A: Gilt on copper
  B: Gilt on brass
Ref.: Babin 39-6, Cox 901

Note: Seven makers of this cap badge exist. Some are identified.

Badge No.	Insignia	Rank	Description	Extremely Fine
125-1-1-2	Cap	ORs	Copper	20.00
125-1-1-4		ORs	Brass	20.00
125-1-1-21		Officers	Gilt on copper	50.00
125-1-1-23		Officers	Gilt on brass	50.00
125-1-1-41	Collars	ORs	Copper	18.00
125-1-1-43		ORs	Brass	18.00
125-1-1-61		Officers	Gilt on copper	20.00
125-1-1-63		Officers	Gilt on brass	20.00
125-1-1-91	Shoulders	ORs	Title: "COC;" Caron	10.00
125-1-1-93		ORs	Title: "COC;" Gaunt	10.00

No.: 125-3-1   **CANADIAN ARMS INSPECTION REPAIR DEPOT**

C.A.I.R.D.

Makers: Unknown
Fasteners: Lugs
Composition:
  Other Ranks: Browning copper
      Officers: Unknown
Ref.: Babin 39-9, Cox 903

Badge No.	Insignia	Rank	Description	Extremely Fine
125-3-1-2	Cap	ORs	Browning copper	150.00
125-3-1-21		Officers	Unknown	--
125-3-1-41	Collars	ORs	Browning copper	75.00
125-3-1-61		Officers	Unknown	--

THE ROYAL CANADIAN POSTAL CORPS

CANADIAN POSTAL CORPS

The Royal Canadian Postal Corps was organized on August 6, 1914. Its staff was drawn from the personnel of the Canadian Postal Corps of the N.P.A.M., formed on May 3, 1911.

No.: 130-1-1

GENERAL SERVICE BADGE

CYPHER "CPC"

Makers: Unknown
Fasteners: Lugs
Composition:
Other Ranks: Copper; brass
Officers:
    A: Gilt copper
    B: Gilt brass
Ref.: Babin 39-4, Cox 936

Badge No.	Insignia	Rank	Description	Extremely Fine
130-1-1-2	Cap	ORs	Copper	45.00
130-1-1-4		ORs	Brass	45.00
130-1-1-21		Officers	Gilt copper	100.00
130-1-1-23		Officers	Gilt brass	100.00
130-1-1-41	Collars	ORs	Copper	35.00
130-1-1-43		ORs	Brass	35.00
130-1-1-61		Officers	Copper	40.00
130-1-1-63		Officers	Brass	45.00
130-1-1-91	Shoulders	ORs	Title: "CPC"	35.00

THE ROYAL FLYING CORPS

By the time of the armistice in France over 13,000 Canadians had served in the Royal Flying Corps.

Some of the badges were made by British companies; however, only those produced by Canadian manufacturers are listed below.

No.: 135-1-1 **GENERAL SERVICE BADGE**

CYPHER "RFC"

Makers: Birks, Roden, Unknown
Fasteners: Lugs
Composition:
  Other Ranks: Browning copper; Brass
  Officers: Gilt on copper
Ref.: Babin

Badge No.	Insignia	Rank	Description	Extremely Fine
135-1-1-2	Cap	ORs	Browning copper; Birks	75.00
135-1-1-4		ORs	Brass, Roden	65.00
135-1-1-21		Officers	Gilt on copper	45.00
135-1-1-41	Collars	ORs	Brass, Roden	50.00
135-1-1-61		Officers	Gilt on copper	65.00
135-1-1-91	Shoulders	ORs	Unknown	--

THE ROYAL REGIMENT OF CANADIAN ARTILLERY

THE ROYAL CANADIAN GARRISON ARTILLERY
(Canadian Garrison Artillery)

No.: 140-1-1

GENERAL SERVICE BADGES
IMPERIAL ISSUE

UBIQUE/QUO FAS ET GLORIA DUCUNT

Makers: Various
Fasteners: Lugs, slide
Composition:
 Other Ranks: Browning copper
 Officers: Browning copper
Ref.: Not previously listed

Note: The officers' issue has a moving wheel on the gun carriage.

Badge No.	Insignia	Rank	Description	Extremely Fine
140-1-1-2	Cap	ORs	Browning copper	15.00
140-1-1-21		Officers	Browning copper	20.00
		Granade Type		
140-1-1-41	Collars	ORs	Browning copper	10.00
140-1-1-43		ORs	Browning brass	10.00
140-1-1-61		Officers	Browning copper	15.00

No. - 140-1-2   **MODIFIED IMPERIAL ISSUE**

CANADA SCROLL OVERLAID ON UBIQUE

With insufficient time to produce new dies, Gaunt produced a Canada scroll and overlaid it on the "UBIQUE" on three different Imperial Gun badge issues — those of Great Britain, the Territorial Army and New Zealand — to produce a Canadian badge.

CANADA/QUO FAS ET GLORIA DUCUNT

Makers: Gaunt
Fasteners: Lugs, slide
Composition:
  Other Ranks: Brass
  Officers: Unknown
Ref.: Not previously listed

Badge No.	Insignia	Rank	Description	Extremely Fine
140-1-2-2	Cap	ORs	Brass "Canada" overlaid on GB	50.00
140-1-2-4		ORs	Brass "Canada" overlaid on TA	100.00
140-1-2-6		ORs	Brass "Canada" overlaid on NZ	100.00
140-1-2-21		Officers	Unknown	- -

THE ROYAL REGIMENT OF CANADIAN ARTILLERY • 195

No. - 140-1-3

CANADIAN ISSUE — STYLE A

GUN WITHOUT WREATH OF MAPLE LEAVES

CANADA/QUO FAS ET GLORIA DUCUNT

Makers: Caron, Gaunt, Tiptaft
Fastener: Lugs, slides
Composition:
  Other Ranks: Browning copper or brass
  Officers: Browning copper
Ref.: Babin 16-1, Cox 331

Note: The officers' issue has a moving wheel on the gun carriage. Not all makers are listed. Badge No. 183C-2 was issued with a movable wheel and slide fastener.

Badge No.	Insignia	Rank	Description	Extremely Fine
140-1-3-2	Cap	ORs	Pickled brass; Unknown	25.00
140-1-3-4		ORs	Browning copper; Caron	25.00
140-1-3-6		ORs	Browning brass; Gaunt	25.00
140-1-3-8		ORs	Browning brass; Tiptaft	25.00
140-1-3-21		Officers	Browning copper; Tiptaft	30.00
	Granade Type			
140-1-3-41	Collars	ORs	Browning copper	10.00
140-1-3-43		ORs	Browning brass	10.00
140-1-3-61		Officers	Browning copper	15.00
	Granade Type with Canada Ribbon			
140-1-3-45	Collars	ORs	Browning copper	15.00
140-1-3-47		ORs	Browning brass; Tiptaft	15.00
140-1-3-63		Officers	Brass; Tiptaft	20.00
	Gun Type			
140-1-3-49	Collars	ORs	Browning copper	15.00
140-1-3-51		ORs	Browning brass; Tiptaft	15.00
140-1-3-65		Officers	Brass; Tiptaft	20.00
140-1-3-91	Shoulders	ORs	Title: "CGA;" Caron	10.00
140-1-3-93		ORs	Title: "CGA;" Ellis	15.00
140-1-3-95		ORs	Title: "R.C.G.A.;" Caron	20.00
140-1-3-97		ORs	Title: "R.C.G.A.;" Ellis	20.00
140-1-3-99		ORs	Title: "R.C.G.A.;" Scully	20.00

No. - 140-1-4 **CANADIAN ISSUE — STYLE B**

GUN WITH WREATH OF MAPLE LEAVES

The wreath design of this badge incorporates four maple leaves on each side of the gun.

CANADA/QUO FAS ET GLORIA DUCUNT

Makers: Unknown
Fasteners: Lugs
Composition:
 Other Ranks: Browning copper
 Officers: Unknown
Ref.: Babin 12-1

Badge No.	Insignia	Rank	Description	Extremely Fine
140-1-4-2	Cap	ORs	Browning copper; Unknown	25.00
140-1-4-21		Officers	Browning copper; Unknown	30.00

THE ROYAL REGIMENT OF CANADIAN ARTILLERY • 197

No. - 140-1-5

CANADIAN ISSUE — STYLE C
GUN WITH TIED WREATH OF MAPLE LEAVES

The wreath design of this badge incorporates five leaves on each side of the gun, plus a tied bow below "Et Gloria."

CANADA/QUO FAS ET GLORIA DUCUNT

Makers: Hemsley
Fasteners: Lugs
Composition:
  Other Ranks: Pickled copper
  Officers: Pickled copper
Ref.: Not previously listed

Badge No.	Insignia	Rank	Description	Extremely Fine
140-1-5-2	Cap	ORs	Pickled copper; Hemsley	50.00
140-1-5-21		Officers	Pickled copper; Hemsley	75.00

No. - 140-1-6 CANADIAN ISSUE - STYLE D

MAPLE LEAF WITH "OVERSEAS"

CANADA/OVERSEAS/QUO FAS ET GLORIA DUCUNT

Makers: Hemsley, Inglis, Service Supply
Fasteners: Lugs
Composition:
  Other Ranks: Browning copper or brass; blackened brass
  Officers: Unknown
Ref.: Babin 12-3, Cox 333

Badge No.	Insignia	Rank	Description	Extremely Fine
140-1-6-2	Cap	ORs	Browning copper; Inglis	50.00
140-1-6-4		ORs	Browning brass; Service Supply	50.00
140-1-6-6		ORs	Blackened brass; Hemsley	50.00
140-1-6-21		Officers	Unknown	- -
140-1-6-41	Collars	ORs	Browning copper; Hemsley	22.00
140-1-6-43		ORs	Browning brass; Service Supply	22.00
140-1-6-45		ORs	Blackened brass; Hemsley	22.00
140-1-6-61		Officers	Unknown	- -

No.: 140-3-1 CANADIAN GARRISION ARTILLERY

MISCELLANEOUS SHOULDER TITLES ONLY

Makers: Various
Fasteners: Lugs
Composition:
  Other Ranks: Copper; Brass
  Officers: Unknown
Ref.: Not previously listed

Badge No.	Insignia	Rank	Description	Extremely Fine
140-3-1	Shoulders	ORs	Title:" 2/CGA"	20.00
140-3-1		ORs	Title: "5/CGA" (greatcoat)	20.00

THE ROYAL CANADIAN FIELD ARTILLERY

CANADIAN FIELD ARTILLERY

No.: 145-1-1

GENERAL SERVICE BADGE
CANADIAN ISSUE — STYLE B
GUN WITH WREATH OF MAPLE LEAVES

The wording "Overseas Field Battery" was added to the rim of the wheel on the gun carriage. Except for this addition this badge is indentical in design to badge no.140-1-5.

CANADA/OVERSEAS FIELD BATTERY/QUO FAS ET GLORIA DUCUNT

Makers: Unknown
Fasteners: Lugs
Composition:
Other Ranks: Pickled copper or brass
Officers: Unknown
Ref.: Babin 12-14

Note: There are four maple leaves on each side of the gun.

Badge No.	Insignia	Rank	Description	Extremely Fine
145-1-1-2	Cap	ORs	Pickled copper	50.00
145-1-1-4		ORs	Pickled brass	50.00
145-1-1-21		Officers	Unknown	- -
145-1-1-41	Collars	ORs	Pickled copper	24.00
145-1-1-43		ORs	Pickled brass	24.00
145-1-1-61		Officers	Unknown	- -
145-1-1-91	Shoulders	ORs	Title: "CROWN/ CFA/CANADA"	10.00
145-1-1-93		ORs	Title: "CFA"	12.00

No.: 145-5-2

MISCELLANEOUS SHOULDER TITLES ONLY

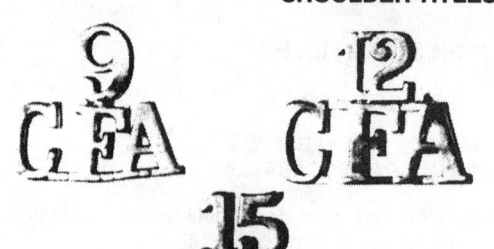

Makers: Various
Fasteners: Lugs
Composition:
 Other Ranks: Copper; brass
 Officers: Unknown
Ref.: Not previously listed

Badge No.	Insignia	Rank	Description	Extremely Fine
145-1-2-91	Shoulders	ORs	Title: "2 C.F.A."	20.00
145-1-2A-93		ORs	Title: "2nd/CFA" (greatcoat)	20.00
145-1-3-91		ORs	Title: "3 C.F.A. Canada," (greatcoat)	20.00
145-1-5-91		ORs	Title: "5 C.F.A."	20.00
145-1-9-91		ORs	Title: "9 C.F.A."	20.00
145-1-9A-93		ORs	Title: "9 C.F.A." (greatcoat)	20.00
145-1-12-91		ORs	Title: "12 C.F.A." (greatcoat)	20.00
145-1-15-91		ORs	Title: "15 C.F.A." (greatcoat)	20.00
145-1-20-91		ORs	Title: "20 C.F.A." (greatcoat)	20.00
145-1-30-91		ORs	Title: "30 C.F.A.," copper	20.00
145-1-30A-93		ORs	Title: "30 C.F.A.," brass	20.00
145-1-33-91		ORs	Title: "33 C.F.A."	20.00
145-1-34-91		ORs	Title: "34 C.F.A.," plain	20.00
145-1-34A-93		ORS	Title: "34 C.F.A.," serifs	20.00
145-1-43-91		ORs	Title: "43 CFA"	20.00

OVERSEAS FIELD BATTERIES

No.: 145-3-13H **13TH BRIGADE HEADQUARTERS**

BRANTFORD AND HAMILTON, ONTARIO

The 13th Brigade Headquarters was organized on March 15, 1915, and disbanded on November 1, 1920.

CANADA/BRIGADE HEADQUARTERS OVERSEAS/13/
QUO FAS ET GLORIA DUCUNT

Makers: Hemsley, Unknown
Fasteners: Lugs
Composition:
  Other Ranks: Pickled copper or brass
  Officers: Pickled brass with silver overlay on design
Ref.: Babin 12-13, Cox 348

STYLE A

STYLE B

STYLE C

Badge No.	Insignia	Rank	Description	Extremely Fine
145-3-13H-2	Cap	ORs	Pickled copper, style A	300.00
145-3-13H-4		ORs	Pickled brass, style B	350.00
145-3-13H-6		ORs	Pickled brass, style C; Hemsley	400.00
145-3-13H-21		Officers	Pickled brass, silver overlay on wheel, Style C; Hemsley	600.00
145-3-13H-41	Collars	ORs	Unknown	--
145-3-13H-61		Officers	Unknown	--
145-3-13H-91	Shoulders	ORs	Unknown	--

No.: 145-3-13A 13TH FIELD ARTILLERY BRIGADE AMMUNITION COLUMN
(BRANTFORD & HAMILTON, ONTARIO)

The 13th Field Artillery Brigade Ammunition Column was organized on July 15, 1916, and disbanded on November 1, 1920.

CANADA/BRIGADE AMMUNITION COLUMN/13/
QUO FAS ET GLORIA DUCUNT

Makers: Hemsley, Unknown
Fasteners: Lugs, tangs
Composition:
  Other Ranks: Pickled brass
  Officers: Pickled brass with silver overlay on design
Ref.: Babin 17-13, Cox 424

STYLE A

STYLE B

Photograph not available

STYLE C

Badge No.	Insignia	Rank	Description	Extremely Fine
145-3-13A-2	Cap	ORs	Pickled brass, style A; Unknown	300.00
145-3-13A-4		ORs	Pickled brass, style B; Unknown	350.00
145-3-13A-6		ORs	Pickled brass, style C; Hemsley	400.00
145-3-13A-21		Officers	Pickled brass, silver overlay on wheel, style C; Hemsley	500.00

THE ROYAL CANADIAN FIELD ARTILLERY • 203

No.: 145-3-36

36TH OVERSEAS FIELD BATTERY

CAPE BRETON, NOVA SCOTIA

CANADA/OVERSEAS FIELD BATTERY/36/
QUO FAS ET GLORIA DUCUNT

Makers: Gaunt, Hemsley, Inglis, Unknown
Fasteners: Lugs, tangs
Composition:
  Other Ranks: Pickled brass
  Officers: Pickled brass and silver
Ref.: Babin, Cox 371

STYLE A

STYLE B

STYLE C

Badge No.	Insignia	Rank	Description	Extremely Fine
145-3-36-2	Cap	ORs	Pickled brass, style A	500.00
145-3-36-4		ORs	Pickled brass, style B	550.00
145-3-36-6		ORs	Pickled brass, style C; Hemsley	600.00
145-3-36-21		Officers	Pickled brass, silver number and hub, style C; Hemsley	600.00
	Maple Leaf Design			
145-3-36-41	Collars	ORs	Pickled brass; Hemsley, Inglis	50.00
145-3-36-61		Officers	Unknown	--
145-3-36-91	Shoulders	ORs	Title: "36 C.F.A;" Gaunt	20.00

204 • THE ROYAL CANADIAN FIELD ARTILLERY

No.: 145-3-38 **38TH OVERSEAS FIELD BATTERY**
SHOULDER TITLE ONLY

Photograph not available

Makers: Unknown
Fasteners: Lugs
Composition:
 Other Ranks: Brass
 Officers: Unknown
Ref.: Not previously listed

Badge No.	Insignia	Rank	Description	Extremely Fine
145-3-38-91	Shoulders	ORs	Brass	25.00

No.: 145-3-46 **46TH OVERSEAS FIELD BATTERY**

QUEENS UNIVERSITY, KINGSTON, ONTARIO

QUEENS C.F.A./46TH

Makers: Unknown
Fasteners: Lugs
Composition:
 Other Ranks: Pickled copper with enamel design
 Officers: Unknown
Ref.: Babin 12-46, Cox

Badge No.	Insignia	Rank	Description	Extremely Fine
145-3-46-2	Cap	ORs	Pickled copper, enamel design	675.00
145-3-46-21		Officers	Unknown	- -
145-3-46-41	Collars	ORs	Unknown	- -
145-3-46-61		Officers	Unknown	- -

50TH OVERSEAS FIELD BATTERY

No.: 145-3-50

QUEEN'S UNIVERSITY, KINGSTON, ONTARIO

CANADA/OVERSEAS FIELD BATTERY/50/
QUO FAS ET GLORIA DUCUNT

STYLE B

STYLE C

Makers: Hemsley, Unknown
Fasteners: Lugs, tangs
Composition:
  Other Ranks: Pickled brass; browning brass
  Officers: Pickled brass and silver
Ref.: Babin 12-50, Cox 385

Note: Style A is not known.

Badge No.	Insignia	Rank	Description	Extremely Fine
145-3-50-2	Cap	ORs	Pickled brass, style B; Unknown	250.00
145-3-50-4		ORs	Pickled brass, style C; Hemsley	200.00
145-3-50-21		Officers	Pickled brass, silver number and hub, style C; Hemsley	400.00
	Garter Design			
145-3-50-41	Collars	ORs	Browning brass; Unknown	150.00
145-3-50-61		Officers	Unknown	--
145-3-50-91	Shoulders	ORs	Title: "Q/50 C.F.A"	45.00
145-3-50-93		ORs	Title: "50 CFA"	30.00

No.: 145-3-51

51ST OVERSEAS FIELD BATTERY

MILITARY DISTRICT 3, KINGSTON, ONTARIO

CANADA/OVERSEAS FIELD BATTERY/51/
QUO FAS ET GLORIA DUCUNT

STYLE B

STYLE C

Makers: Hemsley, Unknown
Fasteners: Lugs, tangs
Composition:
  Other Ranks: Pickled brass
  Officers: Pickled brass and silver
Ref.: Babin 12-51, Cox 386

Note: Style A is not known.

Badge No.	Insignia	Rank	Description	Extremely Fine
145-3-51-2	Cap	ORs	Pickled brass, style B; Unknown	250.00
145-3-51-4		ORs	Pickled brass, style C; Hemsley	200.00
145-3-51-21		Officers	Pickled brass, silver number and hub, style C; Hemsley	400.00

THE ROYAL CANADIAN FIELD ARTILLERY • 207

No.: 145-3-52

52ND OVERSEAS FIELD BATTERY

MILITARY DISTRICT 3, KINGSTON, ONTARIO

CANADA/OVERSEAS FIELD BATTERY/52/
QUO FAS ET GLORIA DUCUNT

Makers: Hemsley, Unknown
Fasteners: Lugs, tangs, pin
Composition:
  Other Ranks: Pickled brass
  Officers:
    A: Pickled copper
    B: Pickled brass and silver
Ref.: Babin 12-52, Cox 387

STYLE B

STYLE C

Note: Style A is not known.

Badge No.	Insignia	Rank	Description	Extremely Fine
145-3-52-2	Cap	ORs	Pickled brass, style B; Unknown	250.00
145-3-52-4		ORs	Pickled brass, style C; Hemsley	200.00
145-3-52-21		Officers	Pickled copper, pin, style B; Unknown	400.00
145-3-52-23		Officers	Pickled brass, silver number and hub, style C; Hemsley	400.00

No.: 145-3-53   **53RD OVERSEAS FIELD BATTERY**

TORONTO, ONTARIO

CANADA/OVERSEAS FIELD BATTERY/53/
QUO FAS ET GLORIA DUCUNT

Makers: Hemsley, Unknown
Fasteners: Lugs, tangs
Composition:
Other Ranks: Pickled brass
Officers: Pickled brass and silver
Ref.: Babin 12-53, Cox 388

STYLE B

STYLE C

Note: Style A is not known.

Badge No.	Insignia	Rank	Description	Extremely Fine
145-3-53-2	Cap	ORs	Pickled brass, Style B	250.00
145-3-53-4		ORs	Pickled brass, Style C; Hemsley	200.00
145-3-53-21		Officers	Pickled brass, Silver number and hub, Style C; Hemsley	400.00
145-3-53-91	Shoulders	ORs	Title: "53 CFA"	25.00

No.: 145-3-55

55TH OVERSEAS FIELD BATTERY

GUELPH, ONTARIO

CANADA/OVERSEAS FIELD BATTERY/55/
QUO FAS ET GLORIA DUCUNT

Makers: Hemsley, Unknown
Fasteners: Lugs, tangs
Composition:
　Other Ranks: Pickled brass
　　Officers: Pickled brass and silver
Ref.: Babin 12-55, Cox 390

STYLE A

STYLE B　　**STYLE C**

Badge No.	Insignia	Rank	Description	Extremely Fine
145-3-55-2	Cap	ORs	Pickled brass, style A; Unknown	250.00
145-3-55-4		ORs	Pickled brass, style B; Unknown	200.00
145-3-55-6		ORs	Pickled brass, style C; Hemsley	150.00
145-3-55-21		Officers	Pickled brass, silver number and hub, style C; Hemsley	400.00
145-3-55-91	Shoulders	ORs	Title: "55CFA"	40.00

56TH OVERSEAS FIELD BATTERY

GUELPH, ONTARIO

STANDARD GUN BADGE

CANADA/OVERSEAS FIELD BATTERY/56/
QUO FAS ET GLORIA DUCUNT

No.: 145-3-56
No. - 145-3-56A

Makers: Hemsley, Unknown
Fasteners: Lugs, tangs
Composition:
  Other Ranks: Pickled brass
  Officers: Pickled brass and silver
Ref.: Babin 12-56, Cox

STYLE A

STYLE B

STYLE C

Badge No.	Insignia	Rank	Description	Extremely Fine
145-3-56A-2	Cap	ORs	Pickled brass, style A; Unknown	250.00
145-3-56A-4		ORs	Pickled brass, style B; Unknown	200.00
145-3-56A-6		ORs	Pickled brass, style C; Hemsley	150.00
145-3-56A-21		Officers	Pickled brass, silver number and hub, style C; Hemsley	400.00
145-3-56A-91	Shoulders	ORs	Title: "56CFA;" Unknown	40.00
145-3-56A-93		ORs	Title: "56/CFA;" Unknown	30.00

MAPLE LEAF BADGE

No. - 145-3-56B

CANADA/OVERSEAS FIELD BATTERY/56/
QUO FAS ET GLORIA DUCUNT

Makers: Inglis
Fasteners: Lugs
Composition:
  Other Ranks: Pickled copper
  Officers: Pickled brass with silver overlay on design
Ref.: Babin 12-56, Cox 391

Note: This is a two-piece badge. The "56" and the battery ribbon are attached to badge number 145-3-64B.

Badge No.	Insignia	Rank	Description	Extremely Fine
145-3-56B-2	Cap	ORs	Pickled copper	350.00
145-3-56B-21		Officers	Pickled brass, Silver overlay on design	500.00
145-3-56B-41	Collars	ORs	Unknown	- -
145-3-56B-61		Officers	Unknown	- -

No.: 145-3-57

57TH OVERSEAS FIELD BATTERY

QUEBEC CITY, QUEBEC

CANADA/OVERSEAS FIELD BATTERY/57/
QUO FAS ET GLORIA DUCUNT

Photograph not available

Makers: Hemsley, Unknown
Fasteners: Lugs, Tangs
Composition:
  Other Ranks: Pickled brass
  Officers: Pickled brass and silver
Ref.: Babin 12-57, Cox 392

STYLE A

STYLE B   **STYLE C**

Badge No.	Insignia	Rank	Description	Extremely Fine
145-3-57-2	Cap	ORs	Pickled brass, style A; Unknown	250.00
145-3-57-4		ORs	Pickled brass, style B; Unknown	200.00
145-3-57-6		ORs	Pickled brass, style C; Hemsley	150.00
145-3-57-21		Officers	Pickled brass, silver number and hub, style C; Hemsley	400.00

No.: 145-3-58

58TH OVERSEAS FIELD BATTERY

Military, District No. 6, Fredricton, New Brunswick

58/CANADA/OVERSEAS BATTERY/CEF

Makers: Hemsley, Unknown
Fasteners: Lugs
Composition:
Other Ranks: Pickled brass
Officers: Pickled brass with silver overlay on design
Ref.: Babin 12-58, Cox 393

Badge No.	Insignia	Rank	Description	Extremely Fine
145-3-58-2	Cap	ORs	Pickled brass; Hemsley	125.00
145-3-58-21		Officers	Pickled brass, silver overlay on design	350.00
145-3-58-41	Collars	ORs	Pickled brass; Hemsley	50.00
145-3-58-61		Officers	Pickled brass, silver overlay on design	100.00

No.: 145-3-61

61ST OVERSEAS FIELD BATTERY
LETHBRIDGE, ALBERTA

CANADA/OVERSEAS BATTERY C.E.F./61/
QUO FAS ET GLORIA DUCUNT

STYLE B

Makers: Hemsley, Unknown
Fasteners: Lugs, tangs
Composition:
 Other Ranks: Pickled brass
 Officers: Pickled brass and silver
Ref.: Babin 12-61, Cox 396

STYLE C

Note: Style A is not known.

Badge No.	Insignia	Rank	Description	Extremely Fine
145-3-61-2	Cap	ORs	Pickled brass, style B; Unknown	250.00
145-3-61-4		ORs	Pickled brass, style C; Hemsley	200.00
145-3-61-21		Officers	Pickled brass, silver number and hub, style C; Hemsley	400.00

62ND OVERSEAS FIELD BATTERY

VICTORIA, BRITISH COLUMBIA

CANADA/OVERSEAS FIELD BATTERY/62/
QUO FAS ET GLORIA DUCUNT

No.: 145-3-62

Makers: Hemsley, Unknown
Fasteners: Lugs, tangs
Composition:
  Other Ranks: Pickled brass
  Officers: PIckled brass and silver
Ref.: Babin 12-62, Cox 397

STYLE A

STYLE B

STYLE C

Badge No.	Insignia	Rank	Description	Extremely Fine
145-3-62-2	Cap	ORs	Pickled brass, style A; Unknown	250.00
145-3-62-4		ORs	Pickled brass, style B; Unknown	200.00
145-3-62-6		ORs	Pickled brass, style C; Hemsley	150.00
145-3-62-21		Officers	Pickled brass, silver number and Hub, style C; Hemsley	400.00

63RD OVERSEAS FIELD BATTERY

LONDON, ONTARIO

No.: 145-3-63

No. - 145-3-63A **STANDARD GUN BADGE**

CANADA/OVERSEAS FIELD BATTERY/63/
QUO FAS ET GLORIA DUCUNT

Makers: Hemsley, Unknown
Fasteners: Lugs, tangs
Composition:
  Other Ranks: Pickled brass
  Officers: Pickled brass and silver
Ref.: Babin 12-63, Cox 398

STYLE A

STYLE B

STYLE C

Badge No.	Insignia	Rank	Description	Extremely Fine
145-3-63A-2	Cap	ORs	Pickled brass, style A; Unknown	250.00
145-3-63A-4		ORs	Pickled brass, style B; Unknown	200.00
145-3-63A-6		ORs	Pickled brass, style C; Hemsley	150.00
145-3-63A-21		Officers	Pickled brass, silver number and hub, style C; Hemsley	400.00
145-3-63A-41	Collars	ORs	Grenade, ribbon, overlaid "63;" Unknown	30.00
145-3-63A-61		Officers	Grenade, overlaid "63;" Unknown	50.00

No. - 145-3-63B **CANADA/63/OVERSEAS**

Photograph not available

Makers: Hemsley
Fasteners: Lugs
Composition:
  Other Ranks: Pickled brass
  Officers: Unknown
Ref.: Not previously listed

Badge No.	Insignia	Rank	Description	Extremely Fine
145-3-63B-2	Cap	ORs	Pickled brass	250.00
145-3-63B-21		Officers	Unknown	--
145-3-63B-41	Collars	ORs	Unknown	--

No.: 145-3-64

No. - 145-3-64A

64TH OVERSEAS FIELD BATTERY
GUELPH, ONTARIO
STANDARD GUN BADGE

CANADA/OVERSEAS FIELD BATTERY/64/
QUO FAS ET GLORIA DUCUNT

Makers: Hemsley, Unknown
Fasteners: Lugs, tangs
Composition:
  Other Ranks: Pickled brass
  Officers: Pickled brass and silver
Ref.: Babin 12-64, Cox 399

STYLE A

STYLE B

STYLE C

Badge No.	Insignia	Rank	Description	Extremely Fine
145-3-64A-2	Cap	ORs	Pickled brass, style A; Unknown	250.00
145-3-64A-4		ORs	Pickled brass, style B; Unknown	200.00
145-3-64A-6		ORs	Pickled brass, style C; Hemsley	150.00
145-3-64A-21		Officers	Pickled brass, silver number and hub, style C; Hemsley	400.00
145-3-64A-91	Shoulders	ORs	Title: "64/C.F.A./CANADA"	30.00

No. - 145-3-64B

MAPLE LEAF BADGE

*CANADA/OVERSEAS/QUO FAS ET GLORIA/
DUCUNT/64/BATTERY*

Makers: Inglis, Unknown
Fasteners: Lugs
Composition:
  Other Ranks: Pickled copper
  Officers: Unknown
Ref.: Babin 12-64, Cox

Note: This is a two-piece badge. The "64" and the battery ribbon have been added to badge number 140-1-6.

Badge No.	Insignia	Rank	Description	Extremely Fine
145-3-64B-2	Cap	ORs	Pickled copper; Inglis	1,000.00
145-3-64B-21		Officers	Unknown	--
145-3-64B-41	Collars	ORs	Unknown	--
145-3-64B-61		Officers	Unknown	--

THE ROYAL CANADIAN FIELD ARTILLERY

No.: 145-3-65

65TH OVERSEAS FIELD BATTERY

WOODSTOCK, ONTARIO

CANADA/OVERSEAS FIELD BATTERY/65/
QUO FAS ET GLORIA DUCUNT

Makers: Hemsley, Unknown
Fasteners: Lugs, tangs
Composition:
  Other Ranks: Pickled brass
  Officers: Pickled brass and silver
Ref.: Babin 12-65, Cox 400

STYLE A

STYLE B

STYLE C

SWEETHEART

Note: Three makers of this cap badge exist:
1. Unknown 1 — solid badge
2. Unknown 2 — void badge, thick numbers
3. Unknown 3 — void badge, thin numbers

Badge No.	Insignia	Rank	Description	Extremely Fine
145-3-65-2	Cap	ORs	Pickled brass, style A; Unknown-1	150.00
145-3-65-4		ORs	Pickled brass, style B, Solid; Unknown-2	200.00
145-3-65-6		ORs	Pickled brass, style B, Void; Unknown-3	200.00
145-3-65-8		ORs	Pickled brass, style C; Hemsley	250.00
145-3-65-21		Officers	Pickled brass, silver number and hub, style C; Hemsley	400.00
145-3-65-91	Shoulders	ORs	Title: "65/CFA/CANADA"	25.00
145-3-65-93	Sweetheart		Pickled copper, pin, style B	25.00

66TH OVERSEAS FIELD BATTERY

MONTREAL, QUEBEC

CANADA/OVERSEAS FIELD BATTERY/66/
QUO FAS ET GLORIA DUCUNT

No.: 145-3-66

Makers: Hemsley, Unknown
Fasteners: Lugs, tangs, pin
Composition:
Other Ranks: Pickled brass
Officers:
  A: Pickled brass
  B: Pickled brass and silver
Ref.: Babin 12-66, Cox 401

Photograph not available

STYLE A

STYLE B   **STYLE C**

Badge No.	Insignia	Rank	Description	Extremely Fine
145-3-66-2	Cap	ORs	Pickled brass, style A; Unknown	250.00
145-3-66-4		ORs	Pickled brass, style B; Unknown	200.00
145-3-66-6		ORs	Pickled brass, style C; Hemsley	150.00
145-3-66-21		Officers	Pickled brass, pin, style B; Unknown	285.00
145-3-66-23		Officers	Pickled brass, silver number and hub, style C; Hemsley	400.00
145-3-66-91	Shoulders	ORs	Title: "C.F.A."	10.00

No.: 145-3-67 **67TH OVERSEAS FIELD BATTERY**

UNIVERSITY OF TORONTO, TORONTO, ONTARIO

CANADA/UNIVERSITY OF TORONTO OVERSEAS/
BATTERY/67/QUO FAS ET GLORIA DUCUNT

Makers: Hemsley, Unknown
Fasteners: Pin, tangs
Composition:
  Other Ranks: Pickled brass
  Officers: Pickled brass and silver
Ref.: Babin12-80, Cox 402

STYLE B

STYLE C

Note: The battery wore the miniature badges as collars. The style A cap badge is not known.

Badge No.	Insignia	Rank	Description	Extremely Fine
145-3-67-2	Cap	ORs	Pickled brass, style B; Unknown	250.00
145-3-67-4		ORs	Pickled brass, style C; Hemsley	200.00
145-3-67-21		Officers	Pickled brass, silver number and hub, style C; Hemsley	400.00
145-3-67-41	Collars	ORs	Pickled copper, style B; Unknown	50.00
145-3-67-61		Officers	Unknown	- -
145-3-67-91	Sweetheart		Pickled copper, pin, style B	25.00

68TH OVERSEAS FIELD BATTERY

VANCOUVER, BRITISH COLUMBIA

CANADA/OVERSEAS FIELD BATTERY/68/
QUO FAS ET GLORIA DUCUNT

No.: 145-3-68

Makers: Hemsley, Unknown
Fasteners: Lugs, tangs
Composition:
  Other Ranks: Pickled brass or copper
  Officers: Pickled brass and silver
Ref.: Babin 12-68, Cox 403

STYLE A

STYLE B

STYLE C

SWEETHEART

Badge No.	Insignia	Rank	Description	Extremely Fine
145-3-68-2	Cap	ORs	Pickled brass, style A; Unknown	250.00
145-3-68-4		ORs	Pickled copper, style B, Unknown	200.00
145-3-68-6		ORs	Pickled brass, style C; Hemsley	150.00
145-3-68-21		Officers	Pickled brass, silver number and hub, style C; Hemsley	400.00
145-3-68-91	Shoulders	ORs	Title: "68 C.F.A."	25.00
145-3-68-93	Sweetheart		Pickled copper, pin, style B	25.00

No.: 145-3-69 — 69TH OVERSEAS FIELD BATTERY

TORONTO, ONTARIO

CANADA/OVERSEAS FIELD BATTERY/69/
QUO FAS ET GLORIA DUCUNT

Makers: Hemsley, Stanley & Aylward, Unknown
Fasteners: Lugs, tangs
Composition:
 Other Ranks: Pickled brass
 Officers: Pickled brass and silver
Ref.: Babin 12-69, Cox 404

STYLE A

STYLE B

STYLE C

Badge No.	Insignia	Rank	Description	Extremely Fine
145-3-69-2	Cap	ORs	Pickled brass, style A; Stanley & Aylward	250.00
145-3-69-4		ORs	Pickled brass, style B; Unknown	200.00
145-3-69-6		ORs	Pickled brass, style C; Hemsley	150.00
145-3-69-21		Officers	Pickled brass, silver number and hub, style C; Hemsley	400.00
145-3-69-91	Sweetheart		Pickled copper, pin, style B	25.00

THE ROYAL CANADIAN FIELD ARTILLERY • 225

No.: 145-3-70

70TH OVERSEAS FIELD BATTERY

TORONTO, ONTARIO

CANADA/OVERSEAS FIELD BATTERY/70/
QUO FAS ET GLORIA DUCUNT

Makers: Hemsley, Unknown
Fasteners: Lugs, tangs
Composition:
  Other Ranks: Pickled brass
  Officers: Pickled brass and silver
Ref.: Babin 12-70, Cox 405

STYLE A

STYLE B

STYLE C

SWEETHEART

Badge No.	Insignia	Rank	Description	Extremely Fine
145-3-70-2	Cap	ORs	Pickled brass, style A; Unknown	250.00
145-3-70-4		ORs	Pickled brass, style B; Unknown	200.00
145-3-70-6		ORs	Pickled brass, style C; Hemsley	150.00
145-3-70-21		Officers	Pickled brass, silver number and hub, style C; Hemsley	400.00
145-3-78-91	Sweetheart		Pickled copper, pin, style B	25.00

No.: 145-3-71   71ST OVERSEAS FIELD BATTERY

ST. CATHARINES, ONTARIO

CANADA/OVERSEAS FIELD BATTERY/71/
QUO FAS ET GLORIA DUCUNT

Makers: Hemsley, Unknown
Fasteners: Lugs, tangs
Composition:
  Other Ranks: Pickled brass
  Officers: Pickled brass and silver
Ref.: Babin 12-71, Cox 406

STYLE B

STYLE C

SWEETHEART

Note: Style A is not known.

Badge No.	Insignia	Rank	Description	Extremely Fine
145-3-71-2	Cap	ORs	Style A; Unknown	--
145-3-71-4		ORs	Pickled brass, style B; Unknown	200.00
145-3-71-6		ORs	Pickled brass, style C; Hemsley	150.00
145-3-71-21		Officers	Pickled brass, silver number and hub, style C; Hemsley	400.00
145-3-71-91	Sweetheart		Pickled copper, pin, style B	25.00

72ND OVERSEAS FIELD BATTERY

No.: 145-3-72

KINGSTON, ONTARIO

CANADA/OVERSEAS FIELD BATTERY/72/
QUO FAS ET GLORIA DUCUNT

STYLE A

Makers: Hemsley, Unknown
Fasteners: Lugs, tangs
Composition:
  Other Ranks: Pickled brass
  Officers: Pickled brass and silver
Ref.: Babin 12-72, Cox 407

STYLE B

STYLE C

SWEETHEART

Badge No.	Insignia	Rank	Description	Extremely Fine
145-3-72-2	Cap	ORs	Pickled brass, style A; Unknown	250.00
145-3-72-4		ORs	Pickled brass, style B; Unknown	200.00
145-3-72-6		ORs	Pickled brass, style C; Hemsley	150.00
145-3-72-21		Officers	Pickled brass, silver number and hub, style C; Hemsley	400.00
145-3-72-91	Sweetheart		Pickled copper, pin, style B	25.00

228 • THE ROYAL CANADIAN FIELD ARTILLERY

No.: 145-3-73   **73RD OVERSEAS FIELD BATTERY**

KINGSTON, ONTARIO

CANADA/OVERSEAS FIELD BATTERY/73/
QUO FAS ET GLORIA DUCUNT

Makers: Hemsley, Unknown
Fasteners: Lugs, tangs
Composition:
  Other Ranks: Pickled brass
  Officers: Pickled brass and silver
Ref.: Babin12-73, Cox 408

STYLE A

STYLE B

STYLE C

SWEETHEART

Badge No.	Insignia	Rank	Description	Extremely Fine
145-3-73-2	Cap	ORs	Pickled brass, style A; Unknown	250.00
145-3-73-4		ORs	Pickled brass, style B; Unknown	200.00
145-3-73-6		ORs	Pickled brass, style C; Hemsley	150.00
145-3-73-21		Officers	Pickled brass, silver number and hub, style C; Hemsley	400.00
145-3-73-91	Sweetheart		Pickled copper, pin, style B	25.00

No.: 145-3-74

74TH OVERSEAS FIELD BATTERY

KINGSTON, ONTARIO

CANADA/OVERSEAS FIELD BATTERY/74/
QUO FAS ET GLORIA DUCUNT

Photograph not available

Makers: Hemsley, Unknown
Fasteners: Lugs, tangs
Composition:
  Other Ranks: Pickled brass
  Officers: Pickled brass and silver
Ref.: Babin 12-74, Cox 409

STYLE A

STYLE B   STYLE C

Badge No.	Insignia	Rank	Description	Extremely Fine
145-3-74-2	Cap	ORs	Pickled brass, style A; Unknown	250.00
145-3-74-4		ORs	Pickled brass, style B; Unknown	200.00
145-3-74-6		ORs	Pickled brass, style C; Hemsley	150.00
145-3-74-21		Officers	Pickled brass, silver number and hub, style C; Hemsley	400.00
145-3-74-91	Sweetheart		Gilt on copper, pin, style B	25.00

No.: 145-3-75   75TH OVERSEAS FIELD BATTERY

KINGSTON, ONTARIO

CANADA/OVERSEAS FIELD BATTERY/75/
QUO FAS ET GLORIA DUCUNT

Makers: Hemsley, Unknown
Fasteners: Lugs, tangs
Composition:
　Other Ranks: Pickled brass
　　　Officers: Pickled brass and silver
Ref.: Bain 12-75, Cox 410

STYLE A

STYLE B

STYLE C

SWEETHEART

Badge No.	Insignia	Rank	Description	Extremely Fine
145-3-75-2	Cap	ORs	Pickled brass, style A; Unknown	250.00
145-3-75-4		ORs	Pickled brass, style B; Unknown	200.00
145-3-75-6		ORs	Pickled brass, style C; Hemsley	150.00
145-3-75-21		Officers	Pickled brass, silver number and hub, style C; Hemsley	400.00
145-3-75-91	Sweetheart		Pickled copper, pin, style B	25.00

76TH OVERSEAS FIELD BATTERY

WINNIPEG, MANITOBA

*CANADA/OVERSEAS FIELD BATTERY/76/
QUO FAS ET GLORIA DECUNT*

No.: 145-3-76

Makers: Hemsley
Fasteners: Lugs
Composition:
  Other Ranks: Pickled brass
  Officers: Picled brass and silver
Ref.: Babin 12-76, Cox 411

Note: Style A and B caps are not known.

Badge No.	Insignia	Rank	Description	Extremely Fine
145-3-76-2	Cap	ORs	Pickled brass, style C; Hemsley	Extremely rare
145-3-76-21		Officers	Pickled brass, silver number and hub, style C; Hemsley	Extremely rare
145-3-76-91	Shoulders	ORs	Title: "76/CFA/CANADA"	40.00
145-3-76-93		ORs	Title: "76 CFA"	40.00

77TH OVERSEAS FIELD BATTERY

REGINA, SASKATCHEWAN

CANADA/OVERSEAS FIELD BATTERY/77/
QUO FAS ET GLORIA DUCUNT

No.: 145-3-77

Makers: Hemsley, Unknown
Fasteners: Lugs, tangs
Composition:
  Other Ranks: Pickled brass
  Officers: Pickled brass and silver
Ref.: Babin 12-77, Cox 412

STYLE B

STYLE C

Note: Style A is not known.

Badge No.	Insignia	Rank	Description	Extremely Fine
145-3-77-2	Cap	ORs	Style A; Unknown	--
145-3-77-4		ORs	Pickled brass, style B; Unknown	200.00
145-3-77-6		ORs	Pickled brass, style C; Hemsley	150.00
145-3-77-21		Officers	Pickled brass, silver number and hub, style C; Hemsley	400.00

THE ROYAL CANADIAN FIELD ARTILLERY • 233

No.: 145-3-78

78TH OVERSEAS FIELD BATTERY

CALGARY, ALBERTA

CANADA/OVERSEAS FIELD BATTERY/78/
QUO FAS ET GLORIA DUCUNT

Photograph not available

Makers: Hemsley, Unknown
Fasteners: Lugs, tangs
Composition:
  Other Ranks: Pickled brass
  Officers: Pickled brass and silver
Ref.: Babin 12-78, Cox 413

STYLE A

STYLE B **STYLE C**

SWEETHEART

Badge No.	Insignia	Rank	Description	Extremely Fine
145-3-78-2	Cap	ORs	Pickled brass, style A; Unknown	250.00
145-3-78-4		ORs	Pickled brass, style B; Unknown	200.00
145-3-78-6		ORs	Pickled brass, style C; Hemsley	150.00
145-3-78-21		Officers	Pickled brass, silver number and hub, style C; Hemsley	400.00
Maple Leaf Design
145-3-78-41	Collars	ORs	Pickled copper	95.00
145-3-78-61		Officers	Unknown	- -
145-3-78-91	Sweetheart		Pickled copper, pin, style B	25.00

79TH OVERSEAS FIELD BATTERY

MONTREAL, QUEBEC

No.: 145-3-79

This was the last field battery formed in Canada.

No. - 145-3-79A   **STANDARD GUN BADGE**

CANADA/OVERSEAS FIELD BATTERY/79/
QUO FAS ET GLORIA DUCUNT

Makers: Hemsley, Unknown
Fasteners: Lugs, tangs
Composition:
  Other Ranks: Pickled brass
  Officers: Pickled brass and silver
Ref.: Babin12-79, Cox 414

STYLE A

STYLE B

STYLE C

SWEETHEART

Badge No.	Insignia	Rank	Description	Extremely Fine
145-3-79A-2	Cap	ORs	Pickled brass, style A; Unknown	250.00
145-3-79A-4		ORs	Pickled brass, style B; Unknown	200.00
145-3-79A-6		ORs	Pickled brass, style C; Hemsley	150.00
145-3-79A-21		Officers	Pickled brass, silver number and hub, style C; Hemsley	400.00
145-3-79A-91	Shoulders	ORs	Title: "79/C.F.A./CANADA"	25.00
145-3-79A-93	Sweetheart		Pickled copper, pin, style B	20.00

No. - 145-3-79B:

GRENADE BADGE

79

Makers: Unknown
Fasteners: Lugs
Composition:
  Other Ranks: Brass
    Officers: Gilt brass with silver overlay
Ref.: Not previously listed

Note: It was worn at Camp Petawawa on the winter fur cap.

Badge No.	Insignia	Rank	Description	Extremely Fine
145-3-79B-2	Cap	ORs	Brass, one piece	500.00
145-3-79B-4		ORs	Brass with "79" overlay	550.00
145-3-79B-21		Officers	Gilt brass with silver "79" overlay	650.00

236 • THE ROYAL CANADIAN FIELD ARTILLERY

TRAINING BATTERIES

The Standard gun badge was worn by training cadets in Valcartier, Quebec, and in England. The training batteries recorded there were numbers 1 to 9 and letters A to D.

No.: 145-5-1

STANDARD GUN BADGE

OVERLAID NUMERAL

Makers: Standard gun badge
Fasteners: Lugs
Composition:
Other Ranks: Standard gun badge with overlaid number or letter
Officers: Unknown
Ref.: Not previously listed

Badge No.	Insignia	Rank	Description	Extremely Fine
145-5-1-1	Cap	ORs	Standard Gun Badge, overlaid "1"	150.00
145-5-1-2		ORs	Standard Gun Badge, overlaid "2"	150.00
145-5-1-3		ORs	Standard Gun Badge, overlaid "3"	150.00
145-5-1-4		ORs	Standard Gun Badge, overlaid "4"	150.00
145-5-1-5		ORs	Standard Gun Badge, overlaid "5"	150.00

THE ROYAL CANADIAN FIELD ARTILLERY • 237

OVERLAID NUMERAL'S CONTINUED

Badge No.	Insignia	Rank	Description	Extremely Fine
145-5-1-6	Cap	ORs	Standard Gun Badge, overlaid "6"	150.00
145-5-1-7		ORs	Standard Gun Badge, overlaid "7"	200.00
145-5-1-8		ORs	Standard Gun Badge, overlaid "8"	200.00
145-5-1-9		ORs	Standard Gun Badge, overlaid "9"	200.00

No. - 145-5-1B   *OVERLAID LETTER*

Maker:
Fasteners: Lugs
Composition:
Other Ranks: Standard gun badge with overlaid letter
Officers: Unknown
Ref.: Not previously listed

Badge No.	Insignia	Rank	Description	Extremely Fine
145-5-1-1A	Cap	ORs	Standard Gun Badge, overlaid "A"	250.00
145-5-1-1B		ORs	Standard Gun Badge, overlaid "B"	250.00
145-5-1-1C		ORs	Standard Gun Badge, overlaid "C"	250.00
145-5-1-1D		ORs	Standard Gun Badge, overlaid "D"	250.00

CANADIAN CORPS HEAVY ARTILLERY

No.: 150-1-3 **3RD OVERSEAS SIEGE BATTERY**

MONTREAL, QUEBEC

No. - 150-1-3A: **WITH "OVERSEAS BATTERY"**

CAN 3 ADA/OVERSEAS BATTERY/SIEGE ARTILLERY/
QUO FAS ET GLORIA DUCUNT

Makers: Inglis
Fasteners: Lugs
Composition:
 Other Ranks: Pickled copper
 Officers: Silver
Ref.: Babin 14-3, Cox

Badge No.	Insignia	Rank	Description	Extremely Fine
150-1-3A-2	Cap	ORs	Pickled copper; Inglis	100.00
150-1-3A-21		Officers	Silver; Inglis	250.00
150-1-3A-41	Collars	ORs	Pickled copper; Inglis	30.00
150-1-3A-61		Officers	Silver; Inglis	75.00

No. - 150-1-3B: **WITHOUT "OVERSEAS BATTERY"**

CANA 3 DIAN/SIEGE BATTERY/QUO FAS ET GLORIA DUCUNT

Makers: Inglis, Tiptaft, Unknown
Fasteners: Lugs
Composition:
 Other Ranks: Pickled copper
 Officers: Unknown
Ref.: Babin 14-3, Cox 425

Note: Two makers of this cap badge exist:
 1. Inglis *(illustrated)* — pointed-leaf design with plain ribbons
 2. Tiptaft — blunt-leaf design with framed ribbons

Badge No.	Insignia	Rank	Description	Extremely Fine
150-1-3B-2	Cap	ORs	Pickled copper; Inglis	150.00
150-1-3B-4		ORs	Pickled copper; Tiptaft	150.00
150-1-3B-21		Officers	Unknown	- -
150-1-3B-41	Collars	ORs	Pickled copper; Inglis	30.00
150-1-3B-43		ORs	Pickled copper; Tiptaft	60.00
150-1-3B-61		Officers	Unknown	- -

No.: 150-1-4 — 4TH OVERSEAS SIEGE BATTERY

CAN 4 ADA/OVERSEAS BATTERY/SIEGE ARTILLERY/ QUO FAS ET GLORIA DUCUNT

Makers: Inglis, Unknown
Fasteners: Lugs
Composition:
  Other Ranks: Pickled copper
  Officers: Unknown
Ref.: Not previously listed

Badge No.	Insignia	Rank	Description	Extremely Fine
150-1-4-2	Cap	ORs	Pickled copper; Inglis	950.00
150-1-4-21		Officers	Unknown	--
150-1-4-41	Collars	ORs	Pickled copper; Inglis	100.00
150-1-4-61		Officers	Unknown	--

No.: 150-1-5 — 5TH OVERSEAS SIEGE BATTERY

CHARLOTTETOWN, PRINCE EDWARD ISLAND

CANADA/OVERSEAS/QUO FAS ET GLORIA DUCUNT/ 5TH SIEGE BATTERY

Makers: Inglis
Fasteners: Lugs
Composition:
  Other Ranks: Pickled copper
  Officers: Pickled copper with white metal overlay on design
Ref.: Babin 14-5

Note: This is a two-piece badge. The "5th" and the "Siege Battery" ribbon are added to the general service badge number 30A.

Badge No.	Insignia	Rank	Description	Extremely Fine
150-1-5-2	Cap	ORs	Pickled copper; Inglis	250.00
150-1-5-21		Officers	Pickled copper, Wm. overlay on design; Inglis	500.00
150-1-5-41	Collars	ORs	Pickled copper; Inglis	100.00
150-1-5-61		Officers	Pickled copper, Wm. overlay on design; Inglis	150.00
150-1-5-63		Officers	Circular badge over "CANADA"	200.00

No.: 150-1-9

9TH OVERSEAS SIEGE BATTERY
SAINT JOHN, NEW BRUNSWICK

The 9th Overseas Seige Battery was organized on July 15, 1916, and disbanded on November 1, 1920.

CANADA/9TH OVERSEAS SIEGE BATTERY/
QUO FAS ET GLORIA DUCUNT

Makers: Hemsley, Unknown
Fasteners: Lugs, tangs
Composition:
 Other Ranks: Pickled brass
 Officers:
  A: Pickled brass with silver overlay on centre design
  B: Gilt on brass
  C: Pickled brass with silver design and hub
Ref.: Babin 14-9, Cox

STYLE B

SWEETHEART

STYLE C

Note: Style A is not known.

Badge No.	Insignia	Rank	Description	Extremely Fine
150-1-9-2	Cap	ORs	Pickled brass, style B; Unknown	250.00
150-1-9-4		ORs	Pickled brass, style C; Hemsley	200.00
150-1-9-21		Officers	Pickled brass, silver overlay on centre design, style B	450.00
150-1-9-23		Officers	Gilt on brass, style B	350.00
150-1-9-25		Officers	Pickled brass, silver design and hub, style C; Hemsley	400.00
150-1-9-91	Sweetheart		Pickled copper, silver overlay, pin, style B	30.00

10TH OVERSEAS SIEGE BATTERY

HALIFAX, NOVA SCOTIA

CANADA/10TH HALIFAX SIEGE BATTERY OVERSEAS/ QUO FAS ET GLORIA DUCUNT

No.: 150-1-10

Makers: Hemsley, Unknown
Fasteners: Lugs, tangs
Composition:
  Other Ranks: Pickled copper or brass
  Officers:
    A: Pickled brass with silver overlay on design
    B: Gilt brass with silver overlay on design
    C: Pickled brass with silver design and hub
Ref.: Babin 14-10, Cox

Photograph not available

STYLE A

STYLE B   STYLE C

Badge No.	Insignia	Rank	Description	Extremely Fine
150-1-10-2	Cap	ORs	Pickled copper, style A; Unknown	250.00
150-1-10-4		ORs	Pickled brass, style B; Unknown	200.00
150-1-10-6		ORs	Pickled brass, style C; Hemsley	250.00
150-1-10-21		Officers	Pickled brass, silver overlay on centre design, style B	400.00
150-1-10-23		Officers	Gilt brass, silver overlay on centre design, style B	400.00
150-1-10-25		Officers	Pickled brass, silver design and hub, style C; Hemsley	400.00

HEAVY ARTILLERY DRAFT BATTERIES

No.: 150-3-5

5TH P.E.I. OVERSEAS SIEGE ARTILLERY DRAFT

CHARLOTTETOWN, PRINCE EDWARD ISLAND

This battery was organized on June 15, 1917, and disbanded on November 1, 1920.

CANADA/SIEGE ARTILLERY DRAFT/
PARVA SUB INCENTI/5/QUO FAS ET GLORIA DUCUNT

STYLE A

Makers: Hemsley, Unknown
Fasteners: Lugs, tangs
Composition:
Other Ranks: Pickled copper or brass
Officers: Pickled brass and silver
Ref.: Babin15-5, Cox

STYLE B

STYLE C

Badge No.	Insignia	Rank	Description	Extremely Fine
150-3-5-2	Cap	ORs	Pickled copper, style A; Unknown	1,200.00
150-3-5-4		ORs	Pickled brass, style B; Unknown	1,100.00
150-3-5-6		ORs	Pickled brass style C; Hemsley	1,200.00
150-3-5-21		Officers	Pickled brass, silver design and hub, style C; Hemsley	1,500.00
150-3-5-41	Collars	ORs	Pickled brass; Unknown	100.00
150-3-5-61		Officers	Pickled brass, silver design and hub, style C; Hemsley	150.00
150-3-5-91	Shoulders	ORs	Annulus with title "CANADA" below; Unknown	150.00

No.: 150-3-7

KING'S COUNTRY
SIEGE ARTILLERY DRAFT

PRINCE EDWARD ISLAND

CANADA/SIEGE ARTILLERY DRAFT/KING'S COUNTY/
PARVA SUB INCENTI/PEI/QUO FAS ET GLORIA DUCUNT

Makers: Unknown
Fasteners: Lugs
Composition:
  Other Ranks: Pickled brass
  Officers: Pickled brass with silver overlay on centre design
Ref.: Not previously listed

Note: Style A and C caps are not known

Badge No.	Insignia	Rank	Description	Extremely Fine
150-3-7-2	Cap	ORs	Pickled brass, style B; Unknown	1,100.00
150-3-7-21		Officers	Pickled brass, silver overlay on centre design, style B; Unknown	1,500.00 1,500.00
150-3-7-41	Collars	ORs	Unknown	- -
150-3-7-61		Officers	Unknown	- -
150-3-7-91	Shoulders	ORs	Annulus with "CANADA" below	200.00

No.: 150-3-9

McGILL UNIVERSITY
OVERSEAS SIEGE ARTILLERY DRAFT

MONTREAL, QUEBEC

No. - 150-3-9A   "OVER SEAS" TWO WORDS

CANADA/UNIVERSITAS COLLEGII McGILL
AD1821/OVERSEAS/GRAND ESCUNT AUCTA LABORE

Makers: Birks, Unknown
Fasteners: Lugs
Composition:
  Other Ranks: Pickled copper or brass
  Officers: Sterling silver
Ref.: Babin 14-1, Cox 422

Badge No.	Insignia	Rank	Description	Extremely Fine
150-3-9A-2	Cap	ORs	Pickled brass; Unknown	125.00
150-3-9A-21		Officers	Sterling silver; Birks	300.00
150-3-9A-41	Collars	ORs	Pickled copper; Unknown	75.00
150-3-9A-43		ORs	Pickled brass; Unknown	75.00
150-3-9A-61		Officers	Sterling silver; Birks	100.00
150-3-9A-91	Sweetheart		Pickled copper, pin	25.00

CANADIAN CORPS HEAVY ARTILLERY

No. - 150-3-9B

"OVERSEAS" ONE WORD

**CANADA/UNIVERSITAS COLLEGII McGILL
AD1821/OVERSEAS/GRAND ESCUNT AUCTA LABORE**

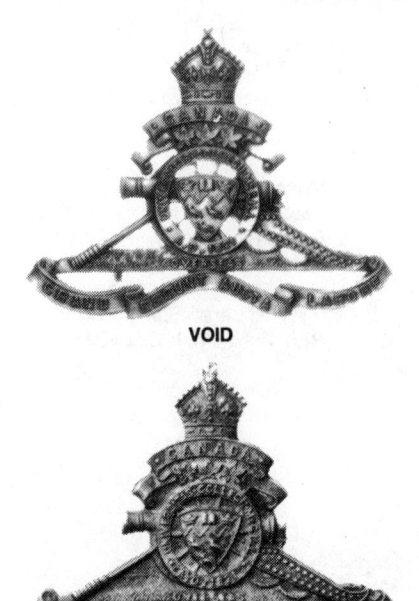

Makers: Birks, Unknown
Fasteners: Lugs
Composition:
 Other Ranks: Pickled brass
  Officers: Sterling silver
Ref.: Babin 14-1, Cox 421 solid, 422 void

VOID

SOLID

Badge No.	Insignia	Rank	Description	Extremely Fine
150-3-9B-2	Cap	ORs	Pickled brass, void; Birks	100.00
150-3-9B-4		ORs	Pickled brass, solid; Birks	100.00
150-3-9B-21		Officers	Sterling silver	250.00
150-3-9B-41	Collars	ORs	Pickled brass, void; Birks	200.00
150-3-9B-43		ORs	Pickled brass, solid; Birks	200.00
150-3-9B-61		Officers	Sterling silver	100.00

No.: 150-3-11

NOVA SCOTIA OVERSEAS SIEGE ARTILLERY DRAFT

HALIFAX, NOVA SCOTIA

The Nova Scotia Overseas Seige Artillery Draft was organized on June 15, 1917, and disbanded on November 1, 1920.

CANADA/SIEGE ARTILLERY DRAFT/NS/
QUO FAS ET GLORIA DUCUNT

Makers: Hemsley, Unknown
Fasteners: Lugs
Composition:
  Other Ranks: Pickled brass
  Officers: Pickled brass with silver overlay on design
Ref.: Not previously listed

STYLE B

Photograph not available

STYLE C

Note: Style A is not known.

Badge No.	Insignia	Rank	Description	Extremely Fine
150-3-11-2	Cap	ORs	Pickled brass, style B; Unknown	1,500.00
150-3-11-4		ORs	Pickled brass, style C; Hemsley	1,500.00
150-3-11-21		Officers	Pickled brass, silver overlay on design, style C; Hemsley	2,000.00

TRENCH MORTAR BATTERIES

Personnel of the Light Trench Mortar Batteries wore the badge of their battalion and the patch of their brigade headquarters with a blue grenade superimposed over it. The 10th and 11th Trench Mortar Batteries each had a special badge, but they were not authorized. It is not known whether they were worn in France.

No.: 150-5-10

No. - 150-5-10A

10TH TRENCH MORTAR BATTERY

MAPLE LEAF DESIGN

10/T.M./BATTERY/CANADA

Makers: Unknown
Fasteners: Lugs
Composition:
 Other Ranks: Browning copper
 Officers: Unknown
Ref.: Babin 20-1, Cox 843

Badge No.	Insignia	Rank	Description	Extremely Fine
150-5-10A-2	Cap	ORs	Browning copper; Unknown	375.00
150-5-10A-21		Officers	Unknown	- -
150-5-10A-41	Collars	ORs	Browning copper; Unknown	200.00
150-5-10A-61		Officers	Unknown	- -

CANADIAN CORPS HEAVY ARTILLERY • 249

No. - 150-5-10B

OVAL DESIGN

***TRENCH MORTAR BATTERY/
OVER 10 SEAS/CANADA***

Makers: Unknown
Fasteners: Lugs, pin
Composition:
  Other Ranks: Browning brass
  Officers: Sterling silver
Ref.: Not previously listed

Badge No.	Insignia	Rank	Description	Extremely Fine
150-5-10B-2	Cap	ORs	Browning brass; Unknown	500.00
150-5-10B-21		Officers	Sterling silver; Unknown	800.00
150-5-10B-41	Collars	ORs	Browning brass; Unknown	200.00
150-5-10B-61		Officers	Sterling silver; Unknown	300.00

No.: 150-5-11

11TH TRENCH MORTAR BATTERY

TRENCH MORTAR BATTERY/OVER 11 SEAS/CANADA

Makers: Unknown
Fasteners: Lugs
Composition:
  Other Ranks: Browning copper
  Officers:
    A: Sterling silver
    B: Gilt on copper
Ref.: Babin 20-2, Cox 844

Badge No.	Insignia	Rank	Description	Extremely Fine
150-5-11-2	Cap	ORs	Browning copper; Unknown	600.00
150-5-11-21		Officers	Sterling silver; Unknown	1,000.00
150-5-11-23		Officers	Gilt on copper; Unknown	500.00
150-5-11-41	Collars	ORs	Browning copper; Unknown	100.00
150-5-11-43		Officers	Sterling silver; Unknown	150.00
150-5-11-45		Officers	Gilt on copper; Unknown	100.00

HEAVY BATTERY DEPOTS

No.: 150-7-1   COBOURG HEAVY BATTERY DEPOT

The Cobourg Heavy Battery Depot was organized on June 15, 1917, and disbanded on November 1, 1920.

CANADA/COBOURG HEAVY BATTERY/OVERSEAS/
C.H.B./QUO FAS ET GLORIA DUCUNT

Makers: Hemsley, Unknown
Fasteners: Lugs, tangs
Composition:
  Other Ranks: Pickled copper or brass
  Officers: Pickled brass with silver overlay on design
Ref.: Babin 13-1, Cox

STYLE A

STYLE B

STYLE C

SWEETHEART

Badge No.	Insignia	Rank	Description	Extremely Fine
150-7-1-2	Cap	ORs	Pickled copper, style A; Unknown	500.00
150-7-1-4		ORs	Pickled brass, style B; Unknown	600.00
150-7-1-6		ORs	Pickled brass, style C; Hemsley	700.00
150-7-1-21		Officers	Pickled brass, silver overlay on wheel; Hemsley	1,000.00
150-7-1-91	Sweetheart		Pickled copper, pin, style B	125.00

CANADIAN CORPS HEAVY ARTILLERY • 251

DIVISIONAL AMMUNITION COLUMNS

No.: 150-9-1   **1ST DIVISIONAL AMMUNITION COLUMN**

CANADA/OVERSEAS FIELD BATTERY/DAC/
QUO FAS ET GLORIA DUCUNT

Makers: Hemsley, Caron
Fasteners: Lugs, tangs
Composition:
Other Ranks: Pickled brass
Officers: Pickled brass with silver overlay on design
Ref.: Babin 17-1, Cox 420

STYLE B

SWEETHEART

Note: This cap was also used for the 2nd, 5th and 8th Divisional Ammunition Columns.

Badge No.	Insignia	Rank	Description	Extremely Fine
150-9-1-2	Cap	ORs	Pickled brass, style B; Unknown	300.00
150-9-1-4		ORs	Pickled brass, style C; Hemsley	350.00
150-9-1-21		Officers	Pickled brass, silver overlay on design, style C; Hemsley	500.00
150-9-1-91	Shoulders	ORs	Title: "DAC;" Caron	10.00
150-9-1-93	Sweetheart		Pickled copper, pin, style B	30.00

No.: 150-9-3   3RD DIVISIONAL AMMUNITION COLUMN

The 3rd Divisional Ammunition Column was organized on July 15, 1916, and disbanded on November 1, 1920.

3RD D.A.C./OVERSEAS/CANADA

Makers: Birks (1916), Unknown
Fasteners: Lugs
Composition:
 Other Ranks: Pickled copper; browning copper
 Officers: Unknown
Ref.: Babin 17-3, Cox 426

Badge No.	Insignia	Rank	Description	Extremely Fine
150-9-3-2	Cap	ORs	Pickled copper; Birks	100.00
150-9-3-4		ORs	Browning copper; Birks	100.00
150-9-3-21		Officers	Unknown	- -
150-9-3-41	Collars	ORs	Unknown	- -
150-9-3-61		Officers	Unknown	- -

No.: 150-9-4   4TH DIVISIONAL AMMUNITION COLUMN

The 4th Divisional Ammunition Column was organized on July 15, 1916, and disbanded on November 1, 1920.

CANADA/OVER 4 SEAS/4TH DIV'N AMMUNITION COL'N

Makers: Birks
Fasteners: Pin, lugs
Composition:
 Other Ranks: Pickled brass
 Officers:
  A: Pickled brass
  B: Browning copper
  C: Sterling silver
Ref.: Babin 17-4, Cox 423

Badge No.	Insignia	Rank	Description	Extremely Fine
150-9-4-2	Cap	ORs	Pickled brass; Birks	75.00
150-9-4-21		Officers	Pickled brass, pin; Birks	75.00
150-9-4-23		Officers	Browning copper, pin; Birks	200.00
150-9-4-25		Officers	Sterling silver, pin; Birks	200.00
150-9-4-41	Collars	ORs	Unknown	- -
150-9-4-61		Officers	Unknown	- -

MISCELLANEOUS

No.: 155-1-1 CANADIAN FIELD COMFORTS COMMISSION

The Canadian Field Comforts Commission was formed at Valcartier, Quebec, in September 1914 and transfered overseas in October 1914. It was a military organization that distributed gifts and voluntary supplies from Canada to Canadian soldiers in the field.

CANADA/F.C.C.

Makers: General list
Fasteners: Lugs
Composition:
Other Ranks: Browning copper with overlay on "F.C.C."
Officers: Unknown
Ref.: Not previously listed

Badge No.	Insignia	Rank	Description	Extremely Fine
155-1-1-2	Cap	ORs	Browning copper, overlay on "F.C.C."	150.00
155-1-1-21		Officers	Unknown	- -
155-1-1-41	Collars	ORs	Unknown	- -
155-1-1-61		Officers	Unknown	- -

No.: 160-1-1 IMPERIAL MUNITIONS BOARD

IMPERIAL MUNITIONSBOARD/ WOMEN WORKERS/CANADA

Makers: Unknown
Fasteners: Pin
Composition: Pickled copper
Ref.: Babin 42-7

Badge No.	Insignia	Description	Extremely Fine
160-1-1	Pin	Pickled copper (six months service bar)	25.00
160-1-1	Bar	With service bars	35.00

No.: 165-1-1   KHAKI UNIVERSITY OF CANADA

The Kharki University of Canada comprised universities thoughout England established for the education of returning soldiers.

KHAKI UNIVERSITY/CANADA

Makers: Unknown
Fasteners: Lugs
Composition:
Other Ranks: Browning copper with white metal overlay on design
Officers: Unknown
Ref.: Babin 42-3, Cox 968

Badge No.	Insignia	Rank	Description	Extremely Fine
165-1-1-2	Cap	ORs	Browning copper, Wm. overlay on design	200.00
165-1-1-21		Officers	Unknown	--
165-1-1-41	Collars	ORs	Browning copper, Wm. overlay on design	100.00
165-1-1-61		Officers	Unknown	--
165-1-1-91	Shoulders	ORs	Unknown	--

Other Titles from our Military Library

The Charlton Standard Catalogue of First World War Canadian Infantry Badges, *2nd Edition*

Five times more badges than the first edition! Use this guide to easily determine the value of the cap, collar and shoulder insignia of Canada's World War I infantry. The manufacturers and the composition of the badges are listed, and the insignia are illustrated throughout. Histories of the battalions are provided, as well as background information for the collector.

432 pages; 5 1/2" x 8 1/2"; softcover; $24.95

The Canadian Medal Rolls - Distinguished Conduct and Military Medal (1939-45 & 1950-53), *By Martin Ashton*

This book confirms the distinguished conduct and military medals awarded to Canadians during World War II and the Korean War. Included is the history of the medals, their warrants by Sir Winston Churchill and the types of awards with typical examples. Verify your medals by the serial numbers, by year of announcement or by an alphabetical index of recipients.

144 pages; 5 1/2" x 8 1/2"; softcover; $19.95

The Canadian Medal Rolls - Distinguished Flying Medal (1939-45), *By Martin Ashton*

A must for all Canadian medal collectors! It's the only book that will verify the D.F.M.s in your collection. It contains the complete roll of recipients of the rare D.F.M., with an informative introduction and history, as well as photographs and technical details.

110 pages; 5 1/2" x 8 1/2"; softcover; $19.95

Medal Roll of the Red River Campaign of 1870 in Canada

The Red River Campaign was dispatched in 1870 to quell the rebellion led by Louis Riel. This book focuses on the Canada general service medal, which was awarded to the participants. Included are a commentary on medal collecting, a summary of the campaign, a detailed description of the C.G.S. medal, the complete roll, notes on related archival records, illustrations and a bibliography.

70 pages; 5 1/2" x 8 1/2"; hardcover; $19.95

Other Titles from our Numismatic Library

The Charlton Standard Catalogue of Canadian Coins, *50th Anniversary Edition*

No other coin catalogue offers so much! It illustrates, describes and prices the entire range of Canadian commercial and commemorative coins from the 1600s to the present. The historical background of each series is provided, as well as a general introduction to Canadian numismatics. Available in English and in French.

275 pages; 5 1/2" x 8 1/2"; softcover; $12.95

The Charlton Standard Catalogue of Canadian Colonial Tokens, *3rd Edition*

A complete guide to the tokens used in Canada between 1794 and 1867. The tokens of Upper Canada, Lower Canada, Prince Edward Island, Nova Scotia, New Brunswick and Newfoundland are all listed and illustrated here, including Canadian blacksmith tokens. Each token is priced and described, including its composition, measurements, date and reference numbers.

272 pages; 5 1/2" x 8 1/2"; softcover; $24.95

The Charlton Standard Catalogue of Canadian Government Paper Money, *8th Edition*

Over 300 years of Canadian paper money. This new edition illustrates and prices all Canadian government paper money from the French colonial issues of 1685 to the current Bank of Canada notes. Army bills, provincial issues, municipal notes, Province of Canada bills, Dominion of Canada issues, special serial numbers and paper money errors are all included.

320 pages; 5 1/2" x 8 1/2"; softcover; $19.95

The Charlton Standard Catalogue of Canadian Bank Notes, *3rd Edition*

More information than in any other book of Canadian bank notes. All the bank notes produced in Canada since the 1700s are in this one easy-to-use, illustrated reference. For this edition a team of numismatic experts has expanded the data and updated the prices.

464 pages; 8 1/2" x 11"; softcover; $59.50

The Charlton Standard Catalogue of Canadian Tire Cash Bonus Coupons, *2nd Edition, by Ross Irwin*

The latest in collectables. Two hundred gas bar and store coupons produced by Canadian Tire since 1958 are described, illustrated and priced in three grades. This catalogue also includes a history of the Canadian Tire Corporation and information on the printing and grading of coupons.

72 pages; 5 1/2" x 8 1/2"; softcover; $14.95